simply Sweet

simply Sweet

LUCY WALLROCK

To my amazing husband Sam. Without you, this would have not
been possible. Thank you for being my best friend, encouraging me
and always saying yes to taste testing!

Contents

FOREWORD

When you look at a menu what's the first thing you look at? Is it the steak, the pasta, the wine? For me, it's easy. I find myself going straight to the sweets (no matter what time of day)! If I could eat only one course for the rest of my life it would be dessert. My last dish would be a chocolate fondant oozing with chocolate lava and served with Crunchie Bar Ice-cream. It's not that I don't like savoury food, on the contrary I love it, but well, I just can't go past sweets!

I spend many a joyful hour pottering in my kitchen, cup of tea in hand, baking cakes and desserts (and of course eating them). It's my happy place, where I feel most content. I came to a realisation that perhaps my happy place should be my work place. After all, you spend so much of your time at work so surely you should love what you do. So after much deliberation I decided to take time out of the 'real world' to try out for MasterChef Australia. A huge fan of the show, I saw it as a fast track to learning as much as I could about food and cooking from the best in the business. So I applied, somehow made it onto the show and a few months later, after some wins (and a fair few disasters), I found myself in the top 10. A while later I was flung back into the real world having finished 6th. I absolutely loved it! It was an amazing journey, one never to be forgotten and, best of all, I learnt so much. What I learnt most however, is that I have so much more to learn.

So after the show when I was contacted to see if I wanted to produce a baking cookbook my immediate reaction was 'no, I can't do it. I'm not a pastry chef. I have so much more to learn before I can produce a book.' However, in the interests of research I spoke to friends and family, asked them what they looked for in a baking cookbook and their answers were unanimous. They didn't have the time, the equipment or the inclination to create sweets worthy of a Michelin star and, after spending most of their cooking time making the savoury 'main' meal, desserts and cakes were a bit of an afterthought, often forgotten and replaced with some chocolates or a plate of fruit. If they were going to make sweets, it had to be easy, simple and worth it. Now that I can help with.

For some, baking is a scary process. This is mainly for three reasons. Firstly, they believe that when baking there can be no room for error in measuring the ingredients. Secondly, that you need lots of expensive equipment that you've never seen before and will most likely use once and never again. And

thirdly, that it is time-consuming. And yes, it can be all of the above but it doesn't need to be. My aim in this book is to make your baking life as easy as possible.

All the ingredients in this book are measured in metric cups and spoons, apart from butter and chocolate which are in grams and this is usually marked in 1¾ oz/50 g increments on the pack itself, so you don't even need to use scales. All you need are measuring cups and spoons, which you can buy in your local supermarket or kitchen shop. I have, however, added ounces and grams so if you don't have metric cups and spoons, and already own a set of scales, you can use these measurements instead.

I have also only included recipes that use equipment that you might already have at home. For instance, I've included recipes for ice-creams but these don't need an ice-cream churner as, if you're anything like me, you will save up for this piece of equipment, use it every weekend for a month and then it will be left in the back of the cupboard collecting dust for the next five years! The one piece of equipment that I can't live without, however, is an electric mixer. It makes baking much easier and quicker, so if you are going to save up for one piece of kitchen equipment, this would be my best bet. However, in the meantime, a cheap electric hand whisk will do.

I also use 'cheat' ways to make sweets quickly and easily, for example my lemon curd uses condensed milk … it's speedier, simpler and to be honest, I think it tastes better. I am certainly not averse to buying readymade pastry. Why spend hours making the perfect sweet flaky pastry when you can buy it in the supermarket instead? And just to show you how easy baking really is, many of the recipes include the classic (Mother) recipe with adapted recipes alongside (Daughter). These show just how easy it is to take a recipe and make it new and exciting with a few extra ingredients. Use these as a starter and then why not create some of your own?

Enclosed are an array of my 'home-style' cakes and desserts for you to try. So now you will have no excuse not to end your meals on a high. After all, sweets are the last memory your guests have of your meal, the one they will remember as the taste lingers, so make it an amazing one.

Tea Time

This is not something that I often admit to, but by about 3PM everyday I have to eat something sweet. I need a sugar fix and I rarely ever go out to buy chocolate bars; instead, I make my own sweet treats.

Of course, I don't admit to my husband (or even myself) that the multitude of homemade biscuits, slices and cakes that precariously balance in the kitchen cupboard are purely for my own benefit (though we both know they are). They are also there to give to guests when they pop by. I mean, you can't offer your guests a cup of tea without something to go with it and why offer a bought biscuit when it's so much nicer to offer them something you've made yourself.

This section is dedicated to a variety of small cakes and slices, larger cakes, cookies and sweets that are quick and easy to make and absolutely sublime to eat. Your guest will mistakenly think you have slaved away for hours so you'll get some serious brownie points, and there may even be a few left over for you too.

Individual Cakes & Slices

Chocolate Brownies

I love chocolate brownies! What is there not to love about a chocolate cake that is soft and moist but also chewy? Could anything be better? What about my Salted Caramel or Peanut Butter Chocolate Brownies? Try these and you will think you've died and gone to brownie heaven!

MOTHER RECIPE

SERVES 8–12 (DEPENDING ON HOW LARGE YOU WANT THE BROWNIE!)

7 oz/200 g unsalted butter, chopped into cubes

1 x 7 oz/200 g bar dark chocolate, broken into pieces

3 eggs

1¼ cups (10½ oz/300 g) superfine/caster sugar

⅔ cup (3½ oz/100 g) all-purpose/plain flour

½ cup (1½ oz/45 g) Dutch cocoa powder

Preheat the oven to 350°F/180°C.

Line a baking tray 11 x 6 in (28 x 17 cm) with baking paper.

Melt the butter and dark chocolate in a saucepan over a low to medium heat, stirring occasionally to ensure the chocolate doesn't burn on the bottom.

Once the chocolate and butter have melted, remove the pan from the heat and let it cool.

Break eggs into a large bowl, add the sugar and whisk by hand until light and fluffy.

When the chocolate mixture is cool, pour the cooled chocolate into the egg mixture, folding together until combined.

Sift in the flour and cocoa powder and stir to combine.

Pour the mixture into the lined baking tray and level the mixture out until flat.

Bake for 30–35 minutes or until cooked. You should be able to stick a sharp knife in it and the knife should come out just about clean. Do not overcook!

Once cooked, remove the brownies from the oven and leave to cool before cutting into desired-sized portions.

White Chocolate and Raspberry Brownies

Preheat the oven to 350°F/180°C.

Line a baking tray 11 x 6 in (28 x 17 cm) with baking paper.

Melt the butter and dark chocolate in a saucepan over a low to medium heat, stirring occasionally to ensure the chocolate doesn't burn on the bottom.

Once the butter and chocolate have melted, remove the pan from the heat and let it cool.

Break eggs into a large bowl, add the sugar and whisk by hand until light and fluffy.

When the chocolate mixture is cool, pour the cooled chocolate into the egg mixture, folding together until combined.

Sift in the flour and cocoa powder and stir to combine. Add the white chocolate and stir thoroughly.

Pour half of the brownie mixture into the baking tray. Dot the raspberries over the top and then pour in the remaining chocolate mixture.

Bake for 30—35 minutes or until cooked. You should be able to stick a sharp knife in it and the knife should come out just about clean. Do not overcook!

Once cooked, remove the brownies from the oven and leave to cool before cutting into desired-sized portions.

7 oz/200 g unsalted butter, chopped into cubes

1 x 7 oz/200 g bar dark chocolate, broken into pieces

3 eggs

1¼ cups (10½ oz/300 g) superfine/caster sugar

2/3 cup (3½ oz/100 g) all-purpose/plain flour

½ cup (1½ oz/45 g) Dutch cocoa powder

¾ cup (5 oz/150 g) white chocolate (very cold and chopped into small pieces)

¾ cup (3½ oz/100 g) whole fresh raspberries

Triple Chocolate Brownies

DAUGHTER RECIPE

SERVES 8—12

7 oz/200 g unsalted butter, chopped into cubes

1 x 7 oz/200 g bar dark chocolate, broken into pieces

3 eggs

1¼ cups (10½ oz/300 g) superfine/ caster sugar

2/3 cup (3½ oz/100 g) all-purpose/ plain flour

½ cup (1½ oz/45 g) Dutch cocoa powder

¾ cup (5 oz/150 g) milk chocolate (very cold and chopped into small pieces)

¾ cup (5 oz/150 g) white chocolate (very cold and chopped into small pieces)

Preheat the oven to 350°F/180°C.

Line a baking tray 11 x 6 in (28 x 17 cm) with baking paper.

Melt the butter and dark chocolate in a saucepan over a low to medium heat, stirring occasionally to ensure the chocolate doesn't burn on the bottom.

Once melted, remove the pan from the heat and let it cool.

Break eggs into a large bowl, add the sugar and whisk by hand until light and fluffy.

When the chocolate mixture is cool, pour the cooled chocolate into the egg mixture, folding together until combined.

Sift in the flour and cocoa powder and stir to combine.

Add the chopped milk and white chocolate and stir thoroughly. Pour the mixture into the lined baking tray and level the mixture out until flat.

Bake for 30—35 minutes or until cooked. You should be able to stick a sharp knife in it and the knife should come out just about clean. Do not overcook!

Once cooked, remove the brownies from the oven and leave to cool before cutting into desired-sized portions.

Peanut Butter Brownies

DAUGHTER RECIPE

SERVES 8—12

Preheat the oven to 350°F/180°C.

Line a baking tray 11 x 6 in (28 x 17 cm) with baking paper.

Melt the butter and dark chocolate in a saucepan over a low to medium heat, stirring occasionally to ensure the chocolate doesn't burn on the bottom.

Once melted, remove the pan from the heat and let it cool.

Break eggs into a large bowl, add the sugar and whisk by hand until light and fluffy.

When the chocolate mixture is cool, pour it into the egg mixture and then fold them together until combined.

Sift the flour and cocoa powder into the mixture and stir to combine.

Pour half of the brownie mixture into the baking tray. Dot the tablespoons of the peanut butter over the mixture and then pour over the remaining chocolate mixture. Level the top of the mixture out so it is flat.

Bake for 30—35 minutes or until cooked. You should be able to stick a sharp knife in it and the knife should come out just about clean. Do not overcook!

Once cooked, remove the brownies from the oven and leave to cool before cutting into desired sized portions.

7 oz/200 g unsalted butter, chopped into cubes

1 x 7 oz/200 g bar dark chocolate, broken into pieces

3 eggs

1¼ cups (10½ oz/300 g) superfine/caster sugar

2/3 cup (3½ oz/100 g) all-purpose/plain flour

½ cup (1½ oz/45 g) Dutch cocoa powder

10 heaped tablespoons peanut butter (crunchy or smooth but not natural peanut butter)

Salted Caramel Brownies

 DAUGHTER RECIPE

SERVES 8–12

1 quantity Salted Caramel Sauce (see recipe page 159)

7 oz/200 g unsalted butter, chopped into cubes

1 x 7 oz/200 g bar dark chocolate, broken into pieces

3 eggs

1¼ cups (10½ oz/300 g) superfine/caster sugar

2/3 cup (3½ oz/100 g) all-purpose/plain flour

½ cup (1½ oz/45 g) Dutch cocoa powder

Make the Salted Caramel.

Preheat the oven to 350°F/180°C.

Line a baking tray 11 x 6 in (28 x 17 cm) with baking paper.

Melt the butter and dark chocolate in a saucepan over a low to medium heat, stirring occasionally to ensure the chocolate doesn't burn on the bottom.

Once melted, remove the pan from the heat and let it cool.

Break eggs into a large bowl, add the sugar and whisk by hand until light and fluffy.

When the chocolate mixture is cool, pour it into the egg mixture and then fold them together until combined.

Sift the flour and cocoa powder into the mixture and stir to combine.

Pour half of the brownie mixture into the baking tray. Dot 10 heaped tablespoons of the salted caramel over the top (it may run all over it if it's not cool enough, which is ok) and then pour over the remaining chocolate mixture.

Bake for 30–35 minutes or until cooked. You should be able to stick a sharp knife in it and the knife should come out just about clean. Do not overcook!

Once cooked, remove the brownies from the oven and leave to cool before cutting into desired-sized portions.

Eccles Cakes

Eccles Cakes remind me of my childhood; my grandmother in particular who always had a few in the pantry for when we came to stay, if only just to keep us quiet for a moment or two. If you've never had them before, you must, they are sublime. Imagine a really flaky sweet pastry surrounding a mixture of sugary currant goodness … sound good? These taste so much better! The traditional way of making Eccles Cakes is with currants but I have included a few other variations.

MOTHER RECIPE

SERVES 12

1 quantity Flaky Pastry (see recipe page 153)

FILLING

¾ oz/25 g unsalted butter

½ cup (2½ oz/75 g) brown sugar

½ cup (2½ oz/75 g) currants

½ teaspoon ground cinnamon

zest of 1 orange, finely grated

milk and superfine/caster sugar, for glazing

Firstly, make the Flaky Pastry.

Preheat the oven to 420°F/220°C.

In a saucepan, melt the butter on a low heat.

Once melted, remove the butter from the heat and stir in the remaining ingredients except the milk and extra sugar for glazing. Leave to cool.

Lightly flour a work surface and roll the flaky pastry dough out to ¼ in (3 mm) thick. Using a 3 in (8 cm) diameter pastry cutter (or a cup) cut the dough into rounds. You should get 12 rounds of dough.

Place about 2 teaspoonfuls of the mixture into the centre of each pastry round. You want it to be full enough that you can just fold the pastry in half and have the two edges meet.

Brush one edge of the pastry with water (you can do this with your finger if you don't have a pastry brush).

Bring up the other side of the pastry and seal it by pinching the edges of the pastry together.

Place the seam of the pastry downwards and, folding the side edges underneath, gently roll the pastry into a ball with your hands. At this stage, all the seams should be underneath the pastry, neatly tucked away.

On a lightly floured bench gently roll the pastry to about ⅛ in (5 mm) thick. Then with your hands gently mould the pastry into a disc shape ⅓ in (1 cm) high.

Line a baking tray with baking paper and place the pastries on the tray about ¾ in (2 cm) apart.

Score 3 diagonal marks with a knife along the top of each pastry. Brush lightly with milk (this can be done with your fingers) and dust with sugar.

Bake for 12–15 minutes or until golden and cooked through.

Once cooked, remove the cakes from the oven and leave to cool before serving.

Walnut and Date Eccles Cakes

DAUGHTER RECIPE

SERVES 12

1 quantity Flaky Pastry (see recipe
   page 153)

FILLING

¾ oz/25 g unsalted butter

½ cup (2½ oz/75 g) brown sugar

¼ cup (1¼ oz/35 g) walnuts, finely
   chopped

½ cup (3 oz/90 g) dates, pitted and
   finely chopped

zest of 1 orange, finely grated

milk and superfine/caster sugar, for
   glazing

Firstly, make the Flaky Pastry.

Preheat the oven to 420°F/220°C.

Melt the butter on a low heat.

Once melted, remove the butter from the heat and stir in the
remaining ingredients except the milk and extra sugar for glazing.
Leave to cool.

Lightly flour a work surface and roll the flaky pastry dough out to
¼ in (3 mm) thick. Using a 3 in (8 cm) diameter pastry cutter (or a
cup) cut the dough into rounds. You should get 12 rounds of dough.

Place about 2 teaspoonfuls of the mixture into the centre of each
pastry round. You want it to be full enough that you can just fold the
pastry in half and have the two edges meet.

Brush one edge of the pastry with water (you can do this with your
finger if you don't have a pastry brush).

Bring up the other side of the pastry and seal it by pinching the
edges of the pastry together.

Place the seam of the pastry downwards and, folding the side edges
underneath, gently roll the pastry into a ball with your hands. At this
stage, all the seams should be underneath the pastry, neatly tucked away.

On a lightly floured bench gently roll the pastry to about $^1/_5$ in
(5 mm) thick. Then with your hands gently mould the pastry into a
disc shape $^1/_3$ in (1 cm) high.

Line a baking tray with baking paper and place the pastries on
them about ¾ in (2 in) apart.

Score 3 diagonal marks with a knife along the top of each pastry.
Brush lightly with milk (this can be done with your fingers) and dust
with sugar.

Bake for 12–15 minutes or until golden and cooked through.

Once cooked, remove the cakes from the oven and leave to cool
before serving.

Figs, Nuts and Seeds Eccles Cakes

DAUGHTER RECIPE

SERVES 12

1 quantity Flaky Pastry (see recipe
   page 153)

FILLING

¼ cup (1¼ oz/35 g) mixed pecans,
   chopped into small pieces, and
   slivered almonds

¼ cup (1½ oz/40 g) mixed pumpkin
   seeds and sunflower kernels

¾ oz/25 g unsalted butter

½ cup (2½ oz/75 g) brown sugar

½ cup (3 oz/90 g) dried figs (chopped
   into ¼ in/5 mm pieces)

zest of 1 orange, finely grated

milk and superfine/caster sugar, for
   glazing

Firstly, make the Flaky Pastry.

Preheat the oven to 350°F/180°C. Place the nuts and seeds on a
lined baking tray and roast for 10–15 minutes or until golden.

Preheat the oven to 420°F/220°C.

Melt the butter on a low heat. Once melted, remove the butter
from the heat and stir in the roasted nuts, figs and remaining
ingredients except the milk and extra sugar for glazing. Leave to cool.

Lightly flour a work surface and roll the flaky pastry dough out to
¼ in (3 mm) thick. Using a 3 in (8 cm) diameter pastry cutter (or a
cup) cut the dough into rounds. You should get 12 rounds of dough.

Place about 2 teaspoonfuls of the mixture into the centre of each
pastry round. You want it to be full enough that you can just fold the
pastry in half and have the two edges meet.

Brush one edge of the pastry with water (you can do this with your
finger if you don't have a pastry brush). Bring up the other side of
the pastry and seal it by pinching the edges of the pastry together.

Place the seam of the pastry downwards and, folding the side edges
underneath, gently roll the pastry into a ball with your hands. All the
seams should be underneath the pastry and neatly tucked away.

On a lightly floured bench, gently roll the pastry to about ¼ in
(5 mm) thick. Then use your hands to gently mould the pastry into a
disc shape ⅓ in (1 cm) high.

Line a baking tray with baking paper and place the pastries on the
tray about ¾ in (2 cm) apart.

Score three diagonal marks with a knife along the top of each
pastry. Brush lightly with milk (this can be done with your fingers)
and dust with sugar.

Bake for 12–15 minutes or until golden and cooked through.
Remove the cakes from the oven and leave to cool before serving.

Chocolate Orange Eccles Cakes

DAUGHTER RECIPE

SERVES 12

1 quantity Flaky Pastry (see recipe
    page 153)

FILLING
¾ cup (5 oz/140 g) dark chocolate
    chips
zest of 1 orange, finely grated
milk and superfine/caster sugar, for
    glazing

Firstly, make the Flaky Pastry.

Preheat the oven to 420°F/220°C.

Mix the chocolate and zest together.

Lightly flour a work surface and roll the flaky pastry dough out to
¼ in (3 mm) thick. Using a 3 in (8 cm) diameter pastry cutter (or a
cup) cut the dough into rounds. You should get 12 rounds of dough.

Place about 2 teaspoonfuls of the mixture into the centre of each
pastry round. You want it to be full enough that you can just fold the
pastry in half and have the two edges meet.

Brush one edge of the pastry with water (you can do this with your
finger if you don't have a pastry brush).

Bring up the other side of the pastry and seal it by pinching the
edges of the pastry together.

Place the seam of the pastry downwards and folding the side edges
underneath, gently roll the pastry into a ball with your hands. At
this stage, all the seams should be underneath the pastry and neatly
tucked away.

On a lightly floured bench gently roll the pastry to about ⅕ in
(5 mm) thick. Then with your hands gently mould the pastry into a
disc shape ⅓ in (1 cm) high.

Line a baking tray with baking paper and place the pastries on the
tray about 1 in (2 cm) apart.

Score 3 diagonal marks with a knife along the top of each pastry.
Brush lightly with milk (this can be done with your fingers) and dust
with sugar.

Bake for 12–15 minutes or until golden and cooked through.

Once cooked, remove the cakes from the oven and leave to cool
before serving.

Lemonade Scones

You can't get much more British then a scone. However, the scones I grew up with can be quite heavy to eat. Not these lemonade scones, which take only minutes to make and are so light and fluffy that one will just never be enough. Best served with clotted cream (or original Chantilly Cream, page 162) and strawberry jam.

MOTHER RECIPE

SERVES 10

2 cups (11 oz/320 g) self-rising/self-raising flour

1 teaspoon baking powder

⅔ cup (5½ oz/165 g) cold lemonade

⅔ cup (6 oz/180 g) single/thickened cream (needs to be 35% less fat)

Preheat the oven to 350°F/180°C.

Sift the flour and baking powder into a large bowl.

Mix the lemonade and cream together, then add the liquid to the flour mixture and stir to combine.

Remove the dough from the bowl and turn out onto a lightly floured surface. Knead the dough gently to form a disc 1 in (2.5 cm) in height. Do not over-knead or the scones will become dense.

Using a pastry cutter 1⅓ in (3.5 cm) in diameter (or an espresso cup if you don't have pastry cutters) cut out rounds of the dough and place these onto a lined baking tray.

Place the tray into the oven and bake for 12–15 minutes or until lightly golden and cooked through.

Once cooked, remove the scones from the oven and leave them to cool before serving.

White Chocolate and Cranberry Scones

DAUGHTER RECIPE

SERVES 10

Preheat the oven to 350°F/180°C.

Sift the flour and baking powder into a large bowl.

Add the cranberries and white chocolate to the bowl.

Mix the lemonade and cream together, then add the liquid to the flour mixture and stir to combine.

Remove the dough from the bowl and turn out onto a lightly floured surface. Knead the dough gently to form a disc 1 in (2.5 cm) in height. Do not over-knead or the scones will become dense.

Using a pastry cutter 1¹/₃ in (3.5 cm) in diameter (or an espresso cup if you don't have pastry cutters) cut out rounds of the dough and place these onto a lined baking tray.

Place the tray into the oven and bake for 12–15 minutes or until lightly golden and cooked through.

Once cooked, remove the scones from the oven and leave them to cool before serving.

2 cups (11 oz/320 g) self-rising/self-raising flour

1 teaspoon baking powder

½ cup (2½ oz/80 g) dried cranberries

½ cup (3½ oz/100 g) white chocolate (chocolate drops or bar chopped into small pieces)

⅔ cup (5½ oz/165 g) cold lemonade

⅔ cup (6 oz/180 g) single/thickened cream (needs to be 35% less fat)

Cinnamon and Raisin Scones

DAUGHTER RECIPE

SERVES 10

2 cups (11 oz/320 g) self-rising/self-
raising flour

1 teaspoon baking powder

1 teaspoon ground cinnamon

½ cup (2½ oz/75 g) currants

⅔ cup (5½ oz/165 g) cold lemonade

⅔ cup (6 oz/180 g) single/thickened
cream (needs to be 35% less fat)

Preheat the oven to 350°F/180°C.

Sift the flour and baking powder into a large bowl. Add in the cinnamon and currants.

Mix the lemonade and cream together, then add the liquid to the flour mixture and stir to combine.

Remove the dough from the bowl and turn out onto a lightly floured surface. Knead the dough gently to form a disc 1 in (2.5 cm) in height. Do not over-knead or the scones will become dense.

Using a pastry cutter 1⅓ in (3.5 cm) in diameter (or an espresso cup if you don't have pastry cutters) cut out rounds of the dough and place these onto a lined baking tray.

Place the tray into the oven and bake for 12–15 minutes or until lightly golden and cooked through.

Once cooked, remove the scones from the oven and leave them to cool before serving.

Chocolate Chip Scones

DAUGHTER RECIPE

SERVES 10

Preheat the oven to 350°F/180°C.

Sift the flour and baking powder into a large bowl. Add the chocolate pieces to the bowl.

Mix the lemonade and cream together, then add the liquid to the flour mixture and stir to combine.

Remove the dough from the bowl and turn out onto a lightly floured surface. Knead the dough gently to form a disc 1 in (2.5 cm) in height. Do not over-knead or the scones will become dense.

Using a pastry cutter $1^1/_3$ in (3.5 cm) in diameter (or an espresso cup if you don't have pastry cutters) cut out rounds of the dough and place these onto a lined baking tray.

Place the tray into the oven and bake for 12–15 minutes or until lightly golden and cooked through.

Once cooked, remove the scones from the oven and leave them to cool before serving.

2 cups (11 oz/320 g) self-rising/self-raising flour

1 teaspoon baking powder

½ cup (3½ oz/100 g) milk or dark chocolate (chocolate drops or bar chopped to small pieces)

⅔ cup (5½ oz/165 g) cold lemonade

2/3 cup (6 oz/180 g) single/thickened cream (needs to be 35% less fat)

Poppy Seed and Orange Scones

DAUGHTER RECIPE

SERVES 10

2 cups (11 oz/320 g) self-rising/self-raising flour

1 teaspoon baking powder

1 tablespoon poppy seeds

zest of 1 orange

⅔ cup (5½ oz/165 g) cold lemonade

⅔ cup (6 oz/180 g) single/thickened cream (needs to be 35% less fat)

Preheat the oven to 350°F/180°C.

Sift the flour and baking powder into a large bowl.

Add the poppy seeds and orange zest to the bowl.

Mix the lemonade and cream together, then add the liquid to the flour mixture and stir to combine.

Remove the dough from the bowl and turn out onto a lightly floured surface. Knead the dough gently to form a disc 1 in (2.5 cm) in height. Do not over-knead or the scones will become dense.

Using a pastry cutter 1⅓ in (3.5 cm) in diameter (or an espresso cup if you don't have pastry cutters) cut out rounds of the dough and place these onto a lined baking tray.

Place the tray into the oven and bake for 12–15 minutes or until lightly golden and cooked through.

Once cooked, remove the scones from the oven and leave them to cool before serving.

These scones are delicious served with Chantilly Cream (page 162) and apricot jam. A match made in heaven!

Banana and Chocolate Chip Muffins

Whether they are eaten for breakfast or tea, these little cakes are always a favourite.

SERVES 18–24 (DEPENDING ON SIZE OF MUFFIN TRAY)

5 oz/150 g unsalted butter, melted, plus extra for greasing

1 cup (8½ oz/240 g) superfine/caster sugar

1 tablespoon golden syrup

2 eggs

6 bananas, mashed

2½ cups (14 oz/400 g) all-purpose/plain flour

½ cup (1½ oz/45 g) cocoa

2 teaspoons baking powder

1 cup (7 oz/200 g) chocolate chips

2 teaspoons baking soda/bicarbonate of soda

½ cup (4 fl oz/125 ml) full-cream milk

Preheat the oven to 375°F/190°C. Grease the muffin tins with butter.

In a large bowl, mix together the sugar, golden syrup, eggs and melted butter until combined.

Add the mashed bananas, flour, cocoa, baking powder and chocolate chips.

Dissolve the baking soda in the milk then fold it into the mixture.

Using a spoon, fill the greased muffin tins with the mixture. It should come almost to the top of each of the muffin trays.

Bake in the oven for 15–20 minutes or until cooked through.

Once cooked, remove the tray from the oven and leave the muffins to cool before serving.

Date Slice

Preheat the oven to 375°F/190°C. Grease and line a 7¾ in (20 cm) square baking tray with baking paper.

To make the base, place the butter and sugars into an electric mixer and using the paddle attachment, on a medium to high speed, cream the butter and sugar together until light and fluffy.

Add the egg and beat well until the ingredients are combined.

Sift the flour, baking soda and salt into the mixer bowl and fold together until thoroughly combined. Form into a dough ball, wrap in plastic wrap and place in the fridge until firm.

Meanwhile for the filling, combine the dates, sugar, golden syrup, cinnamon, lemon juice and zest in a bowl. Leave to stand for 25—30 minutes.

Once the base is firm, remove it from the fridge and press two-thirds of it into the pre-lined tray.

Spread the date mixture evenly over the top.

Crumble the remaining base mix onto the top of the slice and press down lightly to ensure it is compact.

Place the tray in the preheated oven and cook for 20—25 minutes or until the base is cooked through.

Once cooked, remove the tray from the oven and leave to cool in the tray. Once cool, cut the slice into desired-sized fingers or squares and serve.

BASE

4 oz/125 g unsalted butter

½ cup (2½ oz/75 g) brown sugar

½ cup (4 oz/120 g) superfine/caster sugar

1 egg

2 cups (11 oz/320 g) self-rising/self-raising flour

½ teaspoon baking soda/bicarbonate of soda

¼ teaspoon salt

FILLING

3 cups (about 21 oz/600 g) dates, pitted and roughly chopped

2½ tablespoons brown sugar

1 tablespoon golden syrup

1 teaspoon ground cinnamon

juice and zest of 1 lemon

Apricot Flapjacks

(Sticky Oat and Apricot Slices)

I love these chewy oat slices. They are the original muesli bar, though not quite as healthy!

SERVES 18–20

6 oz/175 g unsalted butter

¾ cup (6 oz/180 g) superfine/caster sugar

5 tablespoons golden syrup (if you dip the spoon in hot water the syrup will run off it more easily)

5½ cups (19 oz/550 g) rolled oats

1 cup (9 oz/250 g) apricot jam

Preheat the oven to 350°F/180°C. Grease and line a 8½ in (22 cm) square baking tray with baking paper.

Melt the butter, sugar and golden syrup in a large saucepan over a medium heat. Stir until the butter and sugar have dissolved. Then remove the pan from the heat and stir in the oats, until they are coated in the syrup.

Press half the mixture into the tin with a spoon, level it out and then spread the apricot jam over the top. Cover with the remainder of the oat mixture patting it in tightly with the back of a spoon.

Bake in the oven for 25–30 minutes or until golden.

Once cooked, remove the tray from the oven and leave the flapjack in the tin to cool completely. Once cool, turn out and cut into desired-sized slices.

Millionaire's Shortbread (Caramel Slice)

There are a few steps to this recipe but they are not hard and they are definitely worth it, I promise. Make these for your friends and they will be seriously impressed.

SERVES 20—25

BISCUIT BASE

4 oz/125 g unsalted butter, softened

¼ cup (2 oz/60 g) superfine/caster sugar

1 cup (5½ oz/160 g) all-purpose/plain flour

pinch of salt

CARAMEL CENTRE

4 oz/125 g unsalted butter, chopped

½ cup (4 oz/120 g) superfine/caster sugar

1 tablespoon golden syrup

2 cups (2 x 14 oz/395 g cans) condensed milk

3 tablespoons cold water

CHOCOLATE TOPPING

7 oz/200 g dark chocolate (70% couverture), chopped

Preheat oven to 350°F/180°C.

Line a 8½ in (22 cm) square baking tray with baking paper.

For the biscuit base, place the butter and sugar in an electric mixer and beat on a high speed, with the beater attachment, until the mixture is soft and pale.

Sift in the flour and salt and mix together to form a dough.

Press the dough into the lined baking tray ensuring it is level. Prick the base with a fork all over and bake for 30—35 minutes or until golden. Once cooked, remove the tray from the oven and leave it out to cool.

For the caramel, put the butter, sugar, golden syrup, condensed milk and water into a saucepan.

Stir the mixture over a low heat until the sugar and butter have dissolved. Then bring to the boil and keep on a low boil for 8—10 minutes or until the mixture has turned a caramel colour, stirring continuously.

Remove the pan from the heat and keep stirring until the caramel starts to thicken. Pour the caramel over the shortbread in the tin, level out and then leave to cool until cold.

Break up the chocolate into pieces and melt half in a bowl sitting over a pan of barely simmering water. Once melted, remove from the heat and add the other half of the chocolate, stirring until melted. Then pour the chocolate over the cooled caramel. Place in the fridge to set. Once set, cut into desired-size pieces (mine are usually ¾ in/2 cm square) and serve.

Shared Cakes

Flourless Chocolate Cake with Apricot and Chocolate Frosting

Try this chocolate cake with a twist. It's one not to be missed.

SERVES 8–10

CAKE

7 oz/200 g dark chocolate

5 oz/150 g butter, softened

½ cup (4 oz/120 g) superfine/caster sugar

2 cups (7 oz/220 g) ground almonds

4 eggs, separated

5 tablespoons (7 oz/200 g) apricot jam

ICING

3½ oz/100 g dark chocolate

1¾ oz/50 g butter, softened

Preheat the oven to 350°F/180°C.

Grease and line a 8½ in (22 cm) round cake tin with baking paper.

To make the cake, break the chocolate into small pieces and place in a heatproof bowl sitting over a pan of barely simmering water. Stir until it is melted. Once melted, carefully remove the bowl from the pan and leave it to cool slightly.

Using an electric mixer, cream the butter and sugar together using the beater attachment.

Fold in the ground almonds, egg yolks and melted chocolate to the sugar mixture.

Using an electric mixer whisk the egg whites to stiff peaks, then fold them into the chocolate mixture (a little at a time).

Pour the mixture into the lined cake tin and place it in the oven for 45–50 minutes or until cooked through.

When cooked, remove the cake from the oven and leave it to cool.

Once cool, spread the apricot jam over the top of the cake.

For the icing, melt the remainder of the chocolate and butter and then spread this over the top of the apricot jam.

Let the chocolate icing cool before serving.

Banana Bread

I wasn't introduced to banana bread until after I had left England and I have never looked back! It is a great way to use up some otherwise over-ripe bananas and with the addition of apple this old classic is made even tastier.

SERVES 10–12

2 tablespoons (1¾ oz/50 g) unsalted butter, melted

1 cup (8½ oz/240 g) superfine/caster sugar

1 egg, beaten

3 tablespoons full cream milk

1½ cups (8½ oz/240 g) all-purpose/plain flour

1 teaspoon baking soda/bicarbonate of soda

1 teaspoon baking powder

4 mashed very ripe bananas

1 apple, grated

½ cup (2 oz/55g) walnuts, roughly chopped

1 teaspoon ground cinnamon

Preheat oven to 375°F/190°C. Grease and line a 8½ x 4¾ in (22 x 12 cm) loaf tin with baking paper.

In a large bowl, beat together the butter and sugar until pale. Mix in the egg and milk and stir everything together.

Sift in the flour, baking soda and baking powder and mix to combine.

Gently fold in the mashed banana, grated apple, chopped walnuts and cinnamon.

Pour the mixture into the prepared loaf tin and bake in the oven for 40–50 minutes or until cooked through.

Once cooked, remove the loaf from the oven and leave to cool, on a wire rack, before serving.

Carrot Cake with Lime Frosting

I've tried a few carrot cakes over the past few years and I can't go past this one. It's seriously moist and the tanginess of the lime frosting adds a little something extra.

SERVES 8—10

Preheat the oven to 340°F/170°C.

Grease and line a 8 in (20 cm) round cake tin with baking paper.

Sift the flour, bicarbonate of soda, baking powder and spices into a large bowl.

In a small bowl, lightly whisk the egg and yolk until combined.

In an electric mixer, combine the oil and sugar and at a high speed, using the beater attachment, beat together for 1 minute.

Turn the electric mixer down to low and slowly add the egg mixture, 1 teaspoon at a time, beating until combined.

Remove the bowl from the electric mixer and add the walnuts, coconut, carrot and apple, stirring to combine.

Add the mix of dry ingredients and stir to combine.

Whisk the egg whites until they reach a soft peak.

Gently fold the egg whites into the cake mix. Do not be too vigorous or stir too much, if there are white streaks of the egg whites left running through the mixture do not worry.

Pour the mixture into the lined baking tray, level it flat and put it in the oven for an hour or until cooked through.

Once cooked, remove the cake from the oven and leave to cool.

Recipe cont.

1¼ cups (7 oz/200 g) all-purpose/plain flour

½ teaspoon baking soda/bicarbonate of soda

½ teaspoon baking powder

1 teaspoon cinnamon

¼ teaspoon ground cloves

¼ teaspoon ground ginger

1 whole egg

1 egg yolk

1 cup (9 fl oz/250 ml) sunflower oil

1⅓ cups (11 oz/320 g) superfine/caster sugar

1 cup (4 oz/115 g) walnuts, roughly chopped

¾ cup (2 oz/65 g) desiccated coconut

2 medium carrots, grated (about 4½ oz/130 g)

1 apple, peeled and grated

2 egg whites

10 walnuts, whole, for decoration

FROSTING

5 oz/150 g mascarpone cheese, at
  room temperature

10½ oz/300 g cream cheese, at room
  temperature

¾ cup confectioner's/icing sugar

zest and juice of 2 limes

To make the icing, combine the mascarpone and cream cheese together in an electric mixer and beat on a high speed until soft.

Sift the confectioner's sugar into the mixing bowl and beat until combined fully.

Fold in the lime zest and half the lime juice.

Fold in the remaining lime juice to the desired tangy taste.

Once the cake is cool, spread the frosting onto the top of the cake using a spatula and decorate with the whole walnuts.

Orange, Lemon and Poppy Seed Drizzle Cake

This cake might not look beautiful but don't judge a book by its cover as the sugary lemon and orange syrup makes it unforgettable!

SERVES 10—12

4 oz/120 g unsalted butter, soft

6 oz/175 g self-rising/self-raising flour

¾ cup (6 oz/175 g) superfine/caster sugar

juice and zest of 1 orange

juice and zest of 1 lemon

2 eggs

1 tablespoon poppy seeds

4 tablespoons full cream milk

SYRUP

5 tablespoons confectioner's/icing sugar

juice of 1 lemon

juice of 1 orange

Preheat the oven to 350°F/180°C.

Grease and line a 12 x 5½ in (30 x 14 cm) cake tin with baking paper.

Place the butter, flour, sugar, orange and lemon juice and zest, eggs, poppy seeds and milk in an electric mixer and with the beater attachment, mix until thoroughly combined.

Pour the mixture into the lined baking tin and level the mixture out.

Place in the oven for 35–40 minutes or until cooked through.

Meanwhile, make the syrup. Sieve the confectioner's sugar into a bowl and mix together with the juices from the orange and lemon until the sugar has dissolved (this syrup will run through the cake and make it seriously moist).

Remove the cake from the oven when cooked and, while it is still hot, pierce holes all over the top of the cake with a skewer (or sharp knife).

Pour the syrup over the top of the cake and leave it to cool before removing from the tin and serving.

Easy Fruit Cake

Fruit cakes can be quite testing and time-consuming to prepare but not this one! Best of all, it freezes amazingly well so can be saved (and defrosted) for a rainy day.

SERVES 8—10

2 cups dried mixed fruit (about 15 oz/450 g)

8 oz/225 g butter, diced

1½ cups (12 oz/355 g) superfine/caster sugar

3 eggs, lightly beaten

12 oz/355 g self-rising/self-raising flour

1 teaspoon ground cinnamon

pinch ground cloves

pinch salt

Preheat the oven to 300°F/150°C.

Grease and line a 9½ x 4 in (24 x 11 cm) loaf tin with baking paper.

Place the mixed dried fruit in a large saucepan and just cover with water. Simmer for 5 minutes and then strain off the water. Place the fruit back in the saucepan.

Add the diced butter and sugar to the pan and stir until the butter has melted and the sugar has dissolved. Leave to cool to room temperature.

Once cooled, add the eggs, sift in the flour, spices and salt. Stir together until combined.

Pour the mixture into the lined tin and bake in the centre of the oven for 1 hour and 15 minutes or until cooked through.

Once cooked, remove the loaf from the oven and leave to cool.

Serve with a cup of tea (also lovely with a bit of butter spread on each slice).

Victoria Sponge

There is nothing better than a good old-fashioned sponge cake and this one is the queen of them all.

SERVES 8—10

Preheat the oven to 350°F/180°C.

Grease and line two 8½ in (22 cm) round cake tins with baking paper.

In an electric mixer, beat the butter on a medium speed until it is soft. Gradually add the sugar and keep beating until the mixture is light and fluffy.

In a bowl, gently whisk the eggs together until they are combined.

Beat one spoonful of the beaten eggs at a time into the butter mixture. You will need to do this slowly or it will curdle (if it curdles, add the flour).

Fold the flour and baking powder into the egg mixture.

Add enough warm water to the mixture (a tablespoon at a time, stirring between each) until it reaches dropping consistency. You will know it has reached dropping consistency when you place a bit of batter on a spoon, turn it upside down and the batter just drops off.

Divide the mixture equally between the lined cake tins.

Place the cake tins in the oven and cook for about 25—30 minutes or until the cake has risen, is golden and cooked through.

Remove the cakes from the oven and leave to cool.

Once the cakes are cool, sandwich them together using Chantilly Cream (page 162) and sliced strawberries.

Just before serving, dust the top of the cake with the confectioner's sugar.

8 oz/230 g unsalted butter, softened

1 cup (8½ oz/240 g) superfine/caster sugar

4 eggs

1½ cups (8½ oz/240 g) self-rising/self-raising flour

2 pinches baking powder

4–5 tablespoons warm water

9 oz/250 g strawberries, sliced

confectioner's/icing sugar, sifted for decoration

Chocolate Biscuit Cake (Hedgehog Cake)

This cake is ridiculously easy to make and amazingly rich and delicious. It really does take the biscuit!

SERVES 14—16

16 graham crackers/digestive biscuits
(about 9 oz/250 g)

10½ oz/300 g dark chocolate

9 oz/250 g unsalted butter

3 egg yolks

½ cup (4 oz/120 g) superfine/caster
sugar

2 teaspoons brandy (optional)

Line a 8½ oz (22 cm) square baking tray with baking paper.

Place the biscuits in a zip lock bag and crush roughly with a rolling pin. The biggest pieces should be about ½ in (1.5 cm) in size. Place the broken biscuits into a large bowl.

In a saucepan, melt the chocolate and butter over a low heat. Once melted and combined remove the pan from the heat and allow to cool.

Using a hand whisk, whisk the eggs and sugar together until they are combined and pale.

Once the chocolate is cool, add this and the brandy to the egg mixture and mix until well combined, then pour this mixture over the broken biscuits and gently combine.

Pour the mixture into the lined baking tray, level flat and place into the fridge until set.

Once set, remove the biscuit cake from the fridge and cut it into desired-sized slices and serve.

Cookies

Shortbread

I love the buttery crumbly goodness of shortbread and the following recipes are just a few of my favourite flavours.

MOTHER RECIPE

SERVES 15—20

¼ cup (1¼ oz/35 g) confectioner's/
    icing sugar

9 oz/250 g unsalted butter, softened

1 teaspoon vanilla essence

1½ cups (8½ oz/240 g) all-purpose/
    plain flour

½ cup (2½ oz/70 g) cornstarch/
    cornflour

pinch of salt

Preheat the oven to 400°F/200°C.

Line a large baking tray with baking paper.

Combine the confectioner's sugar, butter and vanilla essence in an electric mixer and beat on a medium speed until light and fluffy.

Sift the flours and salt together into a separate bowl.

Gradually add the dry ingredients to the butter mixture, beating at a low—medium speed until just combined. The mixture will turn to crumbs first and then come together in clumps. At this point stop beating the mixture.

Roll the dough with your hands into a solid log about 1½ in (4 cm) in diameter (the wider it is the bigger your biscuits will be).

Wrap the log tightly in plastic wrap and place in the fridge for 30 minutes or until solid.

When solid, cut the log into ½ in (1 cm) rounds.

Using your hands, quickly so as not to melt the butter, round the edges of the biscuits.

Put the rounds on the lined baking tray, leaving ¾ in (2 cm) between each of them so they have room to expand and then place them in the oven for 20—25 minutes or until lightly golden.

Once cooked, remove the biscuits from the oven and leave them to cool on the baking tray before serving.

Dark Chocolate Halves

¼ cup (1¼ oz/35 g) confectioner's/ icing sugar

9 oz/250 g unsalted butter, softened

1 teaspoon vanilla essence

1½ cups (8½ oz/240 g) all-purpose/ plain flour

½ cup (2½ oz/70 g) cornstarch/ cornflour

pinch of salt

7 oz/200 g dark chocolate (70% couverture), broken into pieces

Preheat the oven to 400°F/200°C.

Line a large tray with baking paper.

Combine the confectioner's sugar, butter and vanilla essence in an electric mixer and beat on a medium speed until light and fluffy.

Sift the flours and salt together into a separate bowl.

Gradually add the dry ingredients to the butter mixture beating at a low–medium speed until just combined. The mixture will turn to crumbs first and then come together in clumps. At this point stop beating the mixture.

Roll the dough with your hands into a solid log about 1½ in (4 cm) in diameter (the wider it is the bigger your biscuits will be).

Wrap the log tightly in plastic wrap and place in the fridge for 30 minutes or until solid.

When solid, cut the log into ½ in (1 cm) rounds.

Using your hands, quickly so as not to melt the butter, round the edges of the biscuits.

Put the rounds on the lined baking tray, leaving ¾ in (2 cm) between each of them so they have room to expand and then place them in the oven for 20–25 minutes or until lightly golden.

Once cooked, remove the biscuits from the oven and leave them to cool on the baking tray.

Put half the chocolate pieces into a heatproof bowl and place over a pan of barely simmering water, stirring until melted. Once melted, remove from the heat and add the remaining chocolate pieces. Stir together until melted.

Dip the cooled biscuits into the melted chocolate, ensuring half the biscuit is covered. Gently shake the excess chocolate off and then place the biscuits on the baking paper. Serve once the chocolate has set.

Chai Shortbread

DAUGHTER RECIPE

SERVES 15—20

¼ cup (1¼ oz/35 g) confectioner's/
  icing sugar

9 oz/250 g unsalted butter, softened

1 teaspoon vanilla essence

1½ cups (8½ oz/240 g) all-purpose/
  plain flour

½ cup (2½ oz/70 g) cornstarch/
  cornflour

pinch of ground cinnamon

pinch of ground cardamom

½ pinch of ground cloves

½ pinch of ground black pepper

pinch of salt

Preheat the oven to 400°F/200°C.

Line a large baking tray with baking paper.

Combine the confectioner's sugar, butter and vanilla essence in an electric mixer and beat on a medium speed until light and fluffy.

Sift the flours, spices and salt together into a separate bowl.

Gradually add the dry ingredients to the butter mixture beating at a low—medium speed until just combined. The mixture will turn to crumbs first and then come together in clumps. At this point stop beating the mixture.

Roll the dough with your hands into a solid log about 1½ in (4 cm) in diameter (the wider it is the bigger your biscuits will be).

Wrap the log tightly in plastic wrap and place in the fridge for 30 minutes or until solid.

When solid, cut the log into ½ in (1 cm) rounds.

Using your hands, quickly so as not to melt the butter, round the edges of the biscuits.

Put the rounds on the lined baking tray, leaving ¾ in (2 cm) between each of them so they have room to expand and then place them in the oven for 20—25 minutes or until lightly golden.

Once cooked, remove the biscuits from the oven and leave them to cool on the baking tray before serving.

Orange and Cranberry Shortbread

DAUGHTER RECIPE

SERVES 15—20

Preheat the oven to 400°F/200°C.

Line a large baking tray with baking paper.

Combine the confectioner's sugar, butter and vanilla essence in an electric mixer and beat on a medium speed until light and fluffy.

Add the orange zest and cranberries and beat on a low speed until just combined.

Sift the flours and salt together into a separate bowl.

Gradually add the dry ingredients to the butter mixture beating at a low—medium speed until just combined. The mixture will turn to crumbs first and then come together in clumps. At this point stop beating the mixture.

Roll the dough with your hands into a solid log about 1½ in (4 cm) in diameter (the wider it is the bigger your biscuits will be).

Wrap the log tightly in plastic wrap and place in the fridge for 30 minutes or until solid.

When solid, cut the log into ½ in (1 cm) rounds. Using your hands, quickly so as not to melt the butter, round the edges of the biscuits.

Put the rounds on the lined baking tray leaving 1 in (2 cm) between each of them so they have room to expand and then place them in the oven for 20—25 minutes or until lightly golden.

Once cooked, remove the biscuits from the oven and leave them to cool on the baking tray before serving.

¼ cup (1¼ oz/35 g) confectioner's/
icing sugar

9 oz/250 g unsalted butter, softened

1 teaspoon vanilla essence

zest of 1 large orange, finely grated

¼ cup (1½ oz/40 g) dried cranberries

1½ cup (8½ oz/240 g) all-purpose/
plain flour

½ cup (2½ oz/70 g) cornstarch/
cornflour

pinch of salt

Pistachio Shortbread

DAUGHTER RECIPE

SERVES 15—20

Preheat the oven to 400°F/200°C.

Line a large baking tray with baking paper.

Combine the confectioner's sugar, butter and vanilla essence in an electric mixer and beat on a medium speed until light and fluffy.

Add the roughly chopped pistachio and beat on a low speed until just combined.

Sift the flours and salt together into a separate bowl.

Gradually add the dry ingredients to the butter mixture beating at a low–medium speed until just combined. The mixture will turn to crumbs first and then come together in clumps. At this point stop beating the mixture.

Roll the dough with your hands into a solid log about 2 in (4 cm) in diameter (the wider it is the bigger your biscuits will be).

Wrap the log tightly in plastic wrap and place in the fridge for 30 minutes or until solid.

When solid, cut the log into ½ in (1 cm) rounds.

Using your hands, quickly so as not to melt the butter, round the edges of the biscuits.

Put the rounds on the lined baking tray, leaving 1 in (2 cm) between each of them so they have room to expand and then place them in the oven for 20–25 minutes or until lightly golden.

Once cooked, remove the biscuits from the oven and leave them to cool on the baking tray before serving.

¼ cup (1¼ oz/35 g) confectioner's/ icing sugar

9 oz/250 g unsalted butter, softened

1 teaspoon vanilla essence

¼ cup (1½ oz/40 g) pistachios, roughly chopped

1½ cup (8½ oz/240 g) all-purpose/ plain flour

½ cup (2½ oz/70 g) cornstarch/ cornflour

pinch of salt

Lemon and Poppy Seed Shortbread

DAUGHTER RECIPE

SERVES 15—20

¼ cup (1¼ oz/35 g) confectioner's/
   icing sugar

9 oz/250 g unsalted butter, softened

1 teaspoon vanilla essence

1 large lemon, finely grated

2 teaspoons poppy seeds

1½ cups (8½ oz/240 g) all-purpose/
   plain flour

½ cup (2½ oz/70 g) cornstarch/
   cornflour

pinch of salt

Preheat the oven to 400°F/200°C.

Line a large baking tray with baking paper.

Combine the confectioner's sugar, butter and vanilla essence in an electric mixer and beat on a medium speed until light and fluffy.

Add the lemon zest and poppy seeds and beat on a low speed until just combined.

Sift the flours and salt together into a separate bowl.

Gradually add the dry ingredients to the butter mixture, beating at a low—medium speed until just combined. The mixture will turn to crumbs first and then come together in clumps. At this point stop beating the mixture.

Roll the dough with your hands into a solid log about 1½ in (4 cm) in diameter (the wider it is the bigger your biscuits will be).

Wrap the log tightly in plastic wrap and place in the fridge for 30 minutes or until solid.

When solid, cut the log into ½ in (1 cm) rounds.

Using your hands, quickly so as not to melt the butter, round the edges of the biscuits.

Put the rounds on the lined baking tray, leaving ¾ in (2 cm) between each of them so they have room to expand and then place them in the oven for 20—25 minutes or until lightly golden.

Once cooked, remove the biscuits from the oven and leave them to cool on the baking tray before serving.

Raisin and Orange Palmiers

These little puff pastry nibbles are quick and easy to make and completely moreish. Once you have the hang of these, try your own fillings, there are so many options.

MAKES 40–50 BITE-SIZED BISCUITS

½ oz/15 g unsalted butter

¼ cup brown sugar

¼ cup currants

zest of ½ orange

¼ teaspoon ground cinnamon

1 sheet ready-rolled puff pastry

milk and superfine/caster sugar, for glazing

Preheat oven to 400°F/200°C.

Line a large baking tray with baking paper.

Melt the butter on a low heat. Once melted, remove the butter from the heat and stir in the sugar, currants, orange zest and cinnamon. Leave to cool.

Cut the puff pastry in half, vertically so you have two long strips.

Spoon and spread the mixture evenly onto the two long strips. Fold the two longest edges on each side in about a quarter of the way towards the middle. Brush the bare pastry with the milk and fold each side over again in the same way. The two folded edges should now be meeting in the middle. Brush well with the milk again.

Wrap the pastry tightly in plastic wrap and place in the fridge for 30 minutes, or for as long as you have until your guests arrive!

Unwrap the pastry and, using a sharp knife, cut the pastry into ¼ in (½ cm) slices. They may look like they are starting to fall apart but keep going as when the pastry puffs out the gaps will be filled. If it is a hot day you might need to do this in batches as the pastry will become hard to work with when warm.

Once cut, lay the pastries (flat-side down) on the pre-lined baking tray about 1 cm apart so they have room to expand.

Cook for 10 minutes or until golden brown and crispy.

Once cooked, remove the biscuits from the oven and serve warm.

Brandy Snaps

These are beautiful rolled and piped full of Date and Orange Cream (page 164), served with Sticky Toffee Puddings (page 106) or shaped into small bowls and filled with Chocolate and Honeycomb Ice-cream (page 136).

MAKES 30

Preheat the oven to 375°F/190°C.

Cut out four separate sheets of baking paper then line a baking tray with them. They need to fit in the baking tray without overlapping and should end up being about 4 x 4 in (10 x 10 cm).

Place the sugar, butter and golden syrup in a saucepan and melt over a medium heat until the butter has melted and the sugar has dissolved.

Remove the pan from the heat and carefully stir in the brandy, being careful as the mixture will froth up a bit.

Leave the mixture to cool to room temperature. This should take about an hour.

Once cooled, sift the flour and ginger into the mixture and stir well to combine.

Place 1 teaspoon of the mixture in the middle of each of the squares of baking paper and bake in the oven for 6–7 minutes or until dark golden.

Once dark golden, remove them from the oven. At this point the biscuits will be soft enough to mould. Working quickly and carefully (they are very hot so you might need to wear gloves), gently place them over a cup to form them into the shape of a bowl or wrap them round a wooden spoon to form a tube. Alternatively you can just leave them flat. When cooled they will become hard and biscuit-like.

Once you have shaped your first four biscuits, repeat the baking and moulding process until all the mixture is used up. You will need to wipe the grease off the baking paper pieces between each batch of biscuits.

½ cup and 1 tablespoon (3¾ oz/110 g) superfine/caster sugar

3½ oz/100 g unsalted butter

4 tablespoons golden syrup

2 tablespoons brandy (can substitute with lemon juice)

¾ cup (3¾ oz/110 g) all-purpose/plain flour

pinch of ground ginger

Coconut, Orange and Date Meringues

A light, chewy, crunchy meringue sandwiched together with flavoured cream (see recipe page 164). A pure delight.

MOTHER RECIPE

SERVES 20

3 egg whites

1 cup (8½ oz/240 g) superfine/caster
  sugar

zest of 1 orange

2 tablespoons cornstarch/cornflour,
  sifted

2 cups (6 oz/172 g) desiccated
  coconut

1 quantity Orange and Date Cream
  (see recipe page 164)

Preheat the oven to 320°F/160°C.

Line a large baking tray with baking paper.

Using an electric mixer whisk the egg whites to soft peaks.

Slowly add the sugar, one tablespoon at a time, to the electric mixer, mixing at a medium speed until all the sugar is combined. At this stage the mixture should be at stiff peak consistency.

Add the orange zest.

Add the sifted flour and dessicated coconut then fold all the ingredients together.

Spoon teaspoons of the mixture onto the lined baking tray. You can use a piping bag if you have one (with a medium nozzle). The meringues need to sit about 1 in (2 cm) apart as they will increase in size.

Place the tray in the oven and bake for 20 minutes or until the meringues are hard on the outside.

Once cooked, remove the meringues from the oven and leave to cool. Keep in an airtight container in the cupboard (not the fridge) until ready for use.

When ready to serve, sandwich two of the meringues together using the Orange and Date Cream (page 164) as the filling.

Coconut, Lemon and Raspberry Meringues

DAUGHTER RECIPE

SERVES 20

Preheat the oven to 320°F/160°C.

Line a large baking tray with baking paper.

Using an electric mixer whisk the egg whites to soft peaks.

Slowly add the sugar, one tablespoon at a time, to the electric mixer, mixing at a medium speed until all the sugar is combined. At this stage the mixture should be at stiff peak consistency.

Add the lemon zest.

Add the sifted flour and dessicated coconut then fold all the ingredients together.

Spoon teaspoons of the mixture onto the lined baking tray. You can use a piping bag if you have one (with a medium nozzle). The meringues need to sit about ¾ in (2 cm) apart as they will increase in size.

Place the tray in the oven and bake for 20 minutes or until the meringues are hard on the outside.

Once cooked, remove the meringues from the oven and leave to cool. Keep in an airtight container in the cupboard (not the fridge) until ready for use.

When ready to serve, sandwich two of the meringues together using the Raspberry Jam Cream (page 167) as the filling.

3 egg whites

1 cup (8½ oz/240 g) superfine/caster sugar

zest of 1 lemon

2 tablespoons cornstarch/cornflour, sifted

2 cups (6 oz/172 g) desiccated coconut

Raspberry Jam Cream (see recipe page 167)

Sweets

Mini Fudge Cookie Squares

Extremely rich fudge squares with a hint of cookie. Try not to eat more than one, I dare you!

MAKES 30—40 SMALL SQUARES

Line a 8½ in (22 cm) square baking tray with baking paper.

In a medium-sized saucepan melt the butter, sugar, condensed milk and golden syrup over a low heat until the butter is melted, the sugar has dissolved and the ingredients combined.

Crush the graham crackers into small pieces using a pestle and mortar (or a rolling pin) and add to the melted ingredients. Mix together until thoroughly combined.

Pour mixture into the lined tray and leave to set in the fridge.

When cool, cut into small squares and serve. If not serving straight away, store the fudge between layers of baking paper in a air-tight container.

4 oz/120 g unsalted butter

¾ cup (6 oz/175 g) superfine/caster sugar

1 x 14 oz/395 g can condensed milk

1 tablespoon golden syrup

16 graham crackers/digestive biscuits (about 9 oz/250 g)

Chocolate Fudge

This recipe reminds me of being at school and experimenting with cooking for the first time. A quick tip for you, to clean the pan once you're done, fill it with water and bring it to the boil then carefully pour the hot water down the sink.

MAKES 20—30 PIECES

2 cups (16 oz/480 g) superfine/caster sugar

2/3 cup (3 oz/90 g) Dutch cocoa powder

4 tablespoons full cream milk

1¾ oz/50 g unsalted butter, cut into cubes

Line a 8½ in (22 cm) square baking tray with baking paper.

Place the sugar, cocoa and milk in a non-stick saucepan and melt over a medium heat, stirring until the sugar has dissolved and the mixture is smooth.

Bring the mixture to the boil, add the butter and stir constantly until the mixture comes to the boil again. Continue to let the mixture boil for 1½ minutes.

Remove the fudge from the heat and keep stirring until it thickens enough to just run off the spoon but isn't runny.

Carefully, pour the fudge into the lined baking tray and place in the fridge to set.

Once set, cut the fudge into desired-sized pieces (be careful not to cut them too big, it is rich) and serve.

Desserts

I personally don't think that there is anything more disappointing than finishing a beautifully prepared main course only to be presented with a mediocre dessert. You are only as good as the last dish you serve to your guests. An average dessert means that all the hard work that has gone into the main and the 'oohs and ahhs' that came with it are suddenly out the window. Dessert is the last flavour you leave your guests with, so don't let all your hard work go to waste, make it a memorable one.

In this section, I have included a variety of individual desserts, shared puddings, ice-creams and petits fours that will leave your guests delighted, satisfied and in awe!

Individual Desserts

Crème Brûlée

I always think of brûlées as being a little decadent and perhaps it is for this reason that I used to think that they were hard to make. Luckily, they are not and even better, once you have mastered the basic Mother Recipe there are so many more flavours you can try, the brûlée world is endless!

MOTHER RECIPE

SERVES 4–6

2 ²/3 cups (16 oz/480 g) single/
    thickened cream
2 vanilla beans (cut in half vertically,
    or 2 teaspoons of vanilla paste)
4 egg yolks
⅓ cup (2½ oz/80 g) superfine/caster
    sugar plus extra, for topping

Preheat the oven to 320°F/160°C.

Put the cream and vanilla into a saucepan and bring to a simmer over a low heat. Then remove the pan from the heat and leave it to sit and infuse for 15 minutes.

Pass the cream mixture through a fine sieve and discard the remnants caught in it.

Whisk the egg yolks and sugar together with a hand whisk until combined.

Add the cream mixture to the saucepan with the sugar mixture (this should now be cool) and whisk together to combine the ingredients.

Pour the mixture equally into the ramekins.

Place the ramekins in a deep baking tray and then carefully, (ensuring no water goes into the ramekins) fill the baking tray with boiling water so it comes three-quarters the way up the ramekins.

Cover the baking tray loosely with tinfoil and place in the oven for 35–45 minutes or until set. The centre of the brûlées should wobble slightly.

Remove the brûlées from the oven and the baking tray and place them in the fridge to cool.

Once cold, add a thin layer of sugar evenly over the top of each of the brûlées and then carefully melt with a blowtorch to create the hard sugar topping. If you do not have a blowtorch you can place the ramekins under a hot grill and grill them for about 5 minutes. Keep an eye on them though as the sugar can turn from caramelised to burnt in an instance. Once you have reached the desired colour, carefully remove the ramekins from the oven and leave them out to cool completely before serving.

Ginger and Orange Brûlée

2²/3 cups (16 oz/480 g) single/
  thickened cream

1 inch knob ginger, grated

zest of 2 oranges

4 egg yolks

⅓ cup (2½ oz/80 g) superfine/caster
  plus extra, for topping

Preheat the oven to 320°F/160°C.

Put the cream and ginger and orange zest into a saucepan and bring to a simmer over a low heat. Then remove the pan from the heat and leave it to sit and infuse for 15 minutes.

Pass the cream mixture through a fine sieve and discard the remnants caught in it.

Whisk the egg yolks and sugar together with a hand whisk until combined.

Add the cream mixture to the saucepan with the sugar mixture (this should now be cool) and whisk together to combine the ingredients.

Pour the mixture equally into the ramekins.

Place the ramekins in a deep baking tray and then carefully (ensuring no water goes into the ramekins) fill the baking tray with boiling water so it comes three-quarters of the way up the ramekins.

Cover the baking tray loosely with tinfoil and place in the oven for 35—45 minutes or until the custard has set. The centre of the brûlées should wobble slightly.

Remove the brûlées from the oven and the baking tray and place them in the fridge to cool.

Once cold, add a thin layer of sugar evenly over the top of each of the brûlées and then carefully melt with a blowtorch to create the hard sugar topping. If you do not have a blowtorch you can place the ramekins under a hot grill and grill them for about 5 minutes. Keep an eye on them though as the sugar can turn from caramelised to burnt in an instance. Once you have reached the desired colour, carefully remove the ramekins from the oven and leave them out to cool completely before serving.

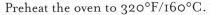

Cinnamon and Cardamom Brûlée

DAUGHTER RECIPE

SERVES 4—6

Preheat the oven to 320°F/160°C.

Lightly crush the cardamom pods and remove the seeds. Grind the seeds to a powder consistency.

Put the cream, cardamom powder and cinnamon stick into a saucepan and bring to a simmer over a low heat. Then remove the pan from the heat and leave it to sit and infuse for 15 minutes.

Pass the cream mixture through a fine sieve and discard the remnants caught in it.

Whisk the egg yolks and sugar together with a hand whisk until combined.

Add the cream mixture to the saucepan with the sugar mixture (this should now be cool) and whisk together to combine the ingredients.

Pour the mixture equally into the ramekins.

Place the ramekins in a deep baking tray and then carefully (ensuring no water goes into the ramekins) fill the baking tray with boiling water so it comes three-quarters of the way up the ramekins.

Cover the baking tray loosely with tinfoil and place in the oven for 35—45 minutes or until the custard has set. The centre of the brûlées should wobble slightly.

Remove the brûlées from the oven and the baking tray and place them in the fridge to cool.

Once cold, add a thin layer of sugar evenly over the top of each of the brûlées and then carefully melt with a blowtorch to create the hard sugar topping. If you do not have a blowtorch you can place the ramekins under a hot grill and grill them for about 5 minutes. Keep an eye on them though as the sugar can turn from caramelised to burnt in an instance. Once you have reached the desired colour, carefully remove the ramekins from the oven and leave them out to cool completely before serving.

6 cardamom pods

2⅔ cups (16 oz/480 g) single/
thickened cream

1 cinnamon stick, broken in half

4 egg yolks

⅓ cup (2½ oz/80 g) superfine/caster
sugar plus extra, for topping

Chocolate Mousse

This mousse is for the chocoholics among you. It's seriously rich, so a little goes a long way!

SERVES 2—4

Melt the chocolate and butter in a saucepan over a medium to low heat, stirring so it doesn't burn on the bottom. Once the chocolate has melted, remove the pan from the heat and leave the chocolate to cool in the pan.

Put the sugar, cream and vanilla into an electric mixer and whisk on a medium speed until soft peaks form.

Add the egg yolk to the cream mixture and stir to combine.

Add the cooled chocolate mixture to the cream and fold together to combine.

Whisk the egg white in the electric mixer until soft peaks form.

Fold the egg white into the chocolate mixture.

Divide the mousse between the ramekins and place in the fridge until they are set (this should take about 1 hour) or until you are ready to serve them.

4 oz/125 g dark chocolate (70% couverture), broken into pieces

⅓ oz/10 g unsalted butter

1 tablespoon superfine/caster sugar

⅔ cup (6 fl oz/180 ml) single/ thickened cream

½ teaspoon vanilla extract

1 egg, separated

Toblerone Mousse

This mousse is light and silky smooth with the added surprise of the nuts and nougat from the Toblerone.

SERVES 4–6

8 oz/225 g Toblerone bar

10 oz/285 ml single/thickened cream

2 egg whites

Break the chocolate into pieces and place in a bowl sitting over a saucepan of barely simmering water. Heat the chocolate until melted, stirring to ensure it doesn't burn. Remove the pan from the heat and the bowl from the pan and leave it to cool.

Whisk the cream in an electric mixer until it forms soft peaks.

Once the chocolate is cool, fold the whipped cream into it.

In a separate bowl, whisk the egg whites until they form soft peaks then fold these into the chocolate mixture as well.

Divide the mixture between ramekins and place them in the fridge until set (this should take between 2–3 hours) or until you are ready to serve them.

Lemon Pots

These pots of delight might be small but they are rich, utterly scrumptious and require very little effort to make.

2 cups (19 fl oz/540 ml) double cream

1 cup (8½ oz/240 g) superfine/caster sugar

zest and juice of 3 lemons

1 cup (9 oz/250 g) raspberries

Place the cream, sugar and lemon zest in a saucepan over a medium heat and bring it to a simmer.

Continue simmering the cream for 3–4 minutes, stirring so it doesn't catch and burn on the bottom of the pan.

Remove the pan from the heat and leave to cool.

Place a few raspberries in each of the ramekins.

Pour the lemon juice into the cooled cream mixture and fold together to combine.

Divide the mixture between the ramekins and then place in the fridge until set or until you are ready to serve them.

Chilli Chocolate Pots

These pots are very chocolatey and rich so I like to serve them in espresso cups as a little goes a long way. They look a little like a mini hot chocolate but with a hot twist.

SERVES 8–10 (SERVED IN ESPRESSO CUPS)

Place the cream and chilli (seeds included) into a saucepan and heat on a low–medium heat until the cream comes to a simmer. Remove the pan from the heat.

Sieve the cream into a clean bowl, discarding the chilli and all of the seeds.

Add the chocolate pieces, a few at a time to start with, to the cream and stir until all the chocolate has melted.

In a separate bowl, lightly whisk together the egg yolks and sugar.

Add the sugar mixture and soft butter to the chocolate and stir well to combine.

Divide the mixture between the espresso cups (or ramekins if you don't have them) and place in the fridge until set. This should take about 2–3 hours.

Garnish with a light sprinkle of chilli flakes and then serve.

1½ cups (10½ fl oz/305 ml) single/ thickened cream

1 bird's eye chilli, halved lengthways, keep seeds

8 oz/200 g dark chocolate (70% couverture), roughly chopped

3 egg yolks

2 tablespoons superfine/caster sugar

¾ oz/25 g unsalted butter, softened

chilli flakes, for decoration

Berry Pots

These little berry pots are incredibly tasty, so I always ensure I make a few more than necessary for extras.

SERVES 4–8 (DEPENDING ON SIZE OF RAMEKINS)

2 cups (17½ oz/500 g) mixed
    berries (strawberries, raspberries,
    blueberries or a mix of them all)
2¼ cups (20 oz/570 g) Greek yoghurt
10 fl oz/285 ml double cream
brown sugar, for topping

If using strawberries, cut them into small pieces (raspberries and blueberries can stay whole).

Divide the berries evenly between the ramekins. The fruit should fill a quarter of each ramekin.

Using a hand beater, lightly whisk the cream until soft peaks form.

Fold the yoghurt and cream together until combined and then spoon the mixture on top of the berries. This should come to about $^1/_3$ in (1 cm) below the top of each of the ramekins.

Spoon the brown sugar on top of the yoghurt mixture so it reaches the top of the ramekins. This needs to be about $^1/_5$–$^1/_3$ in (½–1 cm) in height, which seems a lot but it's worth it.

Place the ramekins in the fridge and leave for about 5 hours or until the sugar has melted. The sugar will form a solid crust a bit like that found on a brûlée. Once the sugar crust has formed they are ready to serve.

Summer Puddings

These individual berry puddings are quintessentially British. They are also really easy to make and are superb served on a hot summer's day with a dollop of Raspberry Jam Cream (page 167) or even Vanilla and Lemon Curd Ice-cream (page 135).

SERVES 6

Lightly spray the inside of 6 ramekins with oil, then cover the inside with plastic wrap, ensuring that there is enough plastic wrap to use as a lid at the end of the process. The oil will help the plastic wrap stick.

Cut the strawberries into small pieces.

Place the berries and sugar into a saucepan and heat over a medium heat for 5 minutes or until the juices begin to run out.

Sieve the berries, reserving the juice and berries separately.

Remove the crusts from the bread and cut the slices into inch-wide fingers.

Dip the bread fingers into the berry juice and line the ramekins with the bread, overlapping each piece until the bread covers the ramekin. Press the edges together so there are no gaps. There will be excess bread hanging over the top; leave these in place.

Spoon the berries into the ramekins, filling them to the top, ensuring they are tightly packed in.

Use the excess bread fingers to cover the berries at the top and then cover tightly with the excess plastic wrap.

Place the ramekins in the fridge for 2–3 hours or until the puddings are completely cold.

Remove the ramekins from the fridge. To turn them out, unwrap the plastic wrap on the top of the ramekins, gently turn them over onto a plate and holding the excess plastic wrap down on the plate pull the ramekin upwards until it comes off. Then gently take the plastic wrap off the puddings.

Spoon over any remaining berries and juice, then dust with confectioner's sugar and serve.

1 lb/500 g raspberries

9 oz/250 g blueberries

9 oz/250 g strawberries

¾ cup (6 oz/180 g) superfine/caster sugar

1 loaf thin to medium sliced white bread

confectioner's/icing sugar, sieved, for decoration

Sticky Toffee Puddings

This is one of my all-time favourite desserts especially on a cold night while snuggled up by the fire. Serve with Brandy Snaps (page 77) and Orange and Date Cream (page 164) if you want to impress your guests.

SERVES 6–8 (DEPENDING HOW LARGE YOUR MUFFIN TRAYS ARE)

1¼ cups (9 oz/250 g) dates, pitted and roughly chopped

1 cup (9 fl oz/250 ml) water

1 teaspoon baking soda/bicarbonate of soda

1 cup (5 oz/150 g) brown sugar

3 oz/85 g unsalted butter, softened

2 eggs

1 cup (5½ oz/160 g) self-rising/self-raising flour

pinch of baking powder

1 quantity Butterscotch Sauce (see recipe page 157)

Orange and Date Cream (see recipe page 164) (optional)

6–8 Brandy Snaps (see recipe page 77) (optional)

Preheat the oven to 350°F/180°C.

Grease 6–8 muffin tins with butter and line the base of them with baking paper rounds.

Put the chopped dates and water into a saucepan. Bring them to the boil over a high heat and then turn the heat down to low and leave to simmer for 5 minutes.

Remove the pan from the heat and stir in the bicarbonate of soda with a wooden spoon until completely combined and a thick paste forms. Leave the date mixture to cool.

In an electric mixer, cream together the butter and sugar, using the beater attachment, until light and pale.

Add the eggs to the mixture and beat thoroughly to combine.

Add the flour to the date mixture and stir thoroughly to combine.

Bake in the oven for 20–30 minutes, or until cooked.

Once cooked, remove the puddings from the oven and turn them out onto individual plates.

Pour the Butterscotch Sauce over the sticky date pudding. You can serve these with a scoop of ice-cream if you like. Or, if you have guests over, add a dollop of Orange and Date Cream and a Brandy Snap to make these truly elegant.

Baked Apples

This is one of the healthier options in this book … granted, there aren't many. If you've got a few leftover apples, then try this deliciously heart-warming dessert made even more so when served with Cardamom and Coconut Ice-cream (page 135), making it not quite so healthy after all!

SERVES 5—6

5–6 apples

1¾ oz/50 g unsalted butter, softened

pinch ground cloves

1 teaspoon ground cinnamon

¾ cup (4 oz/120 g) currants

⅓ cup (1¾ oz/50 g) flaked almonds

zest of 1 orange

zest of 1 lemon

⅔ cup (3½ oz/100 g) brown sugar

⅓ cup (3 oz/85 ml) whisky or brandy
   or orange juice

Preheat oven to 350°F/180°C.

Line a baking tray with baking paper. Core the apples and then score around the middle with a knife

In a bowl, thoroughly combine the butter, spices, currants, almonds, orange and lemon zest, sugar and brandy (or whisky or orange juice).

Fill the cored apples with the mixture making sure it is packed in tightly.

Place the apples on the lined baking tray and spoon over any remaining juices.

Bake in the oven for 35–40 minutes or until the apples are cooked through. Don't worry if they break apart a little.

Once cooked, remove the tray from the oven. Serve the apples warm and make sure to spoon over any leftover sauce. I like to serve this with a dollop of cream.

Shared Desserts

Lemon Meringue Pie

I used to make this pie with real lemon curd but this version using condensed milk is much easier, quicker and I believe tastier. The Sweet Pastry used in this recipe is deliciously light, crumbly and easy to make but if time is of the essence you can always buy shortcrust pastry from the shops.

SERVES 8—10

1 quantity Sweet Pastry (see recipe
    page 152)
1 tablespoon lemon zest

FILLING
zest of 1 large lemon
1 cup (9 fl oz/250 ml) lemon juice
2 x 13½ oz/395 g cans condensed
    milk
2 egg yolks

MERINGUE
3 egg whites
¼ cup (2 oz/60 g) superfine/caster
    sugar

Make the Sweet Pastry with a tablespoon of finely grated lemon zest added to the recipe or buy a pre-made and pre-cooked shortcrust tart case from the shops.

If making your own pastry, blind bake it as per the recipe instructions and leave it to cool in the tin.

Preheat the oven to 320°F/160°C.

Thoroughly mix the lemon zest and juice, condensed milk and egg yolks. Add more lemon juice to taste if desired.

Pour the mixture into the pastry so it almost reaches the top.

To make the meringue, place the egg whites into a clean mixing bowl and whisk on a high speed until soft peaks form. Continue to whisk, adding the sugar a little at a time until all combined.

With a spoon, pile the meringue mixture onto the top of the pastry. Alternatively, you could pipe the meringue mixture on top and swirl it on top of the pie.

Place in the oven and bake for 10 minutes or until the meringue is starting to brown and the curd has set.

Remove from the oven and serve warm.

Lime Pie

SERVES 8—10

1 quantity Sweet Pastry (see recipe
     page 152)

FILLING
zest of 1 large lime
1 cup (9 fl oz/250 ml) lime juice
2 x 14 oz/395 g cans condensed milk
2 egg yolks

Make the Sweet Pastry according to the recipe or buy a pre-made and pre-cooked shortcrust tart case from the shops.

If making your own pastry, blind bake it as per the recipe instructions and leave it to cool in the tin.

Preheat the oven to 320°F/160°C.

Thoroughly mix the lime zest and juice, condensed milk and egg yolks. Add more lime juice to taste if desired.

Pour the mixture into the pastry so it almost reaches the top.

Place in the oven and bake for 10 minutes or until the curd has set. Remove from the oven and allow to cool.

Once cooled, top with piped Chantilly Cream (page 162) and serve.

Chocolate, Pear and Almond Tart

This tart is perfect for a cold winter's day. The outside of the tart will cook but the inside will remain soft, almost sauce-like. A tart that's almost a pudding, what's not to love?! Serve warm with Vanilla Ice-cream (page 134).

SERVES 8—10

You will need to make Sweet Pastry or you can buy shortcrust pastry from the shops or buy a pre-made and pre-cooked shortcrust tart case from the shops.

If making your own pastry, blind bake it as per the recipe instructions and leave it to cool in the tin.

Preheat the oven to 350°F/180°C.

In a saucepan, combine the butter, ground almonds, sugar and chocolate and place over a low—medium heat until melted, stirring occasionally to combine. Once combined, remove the pan from the heat and leave the mixture to cool.

Lightly beat the eggs.

Once the chocolate mixture is cool, add the eggs, one teaspoon at a time, and stir to combine.

Pour the mixture into the pastry case, level out and decorate with the sliced pears.

Put the tart in the oven and bake for 40—45 minutes or until set. The outside will be firm but the centre will remain gooey. Serve this tart warm with perhaps some cream or ice-cream on the side.

1 quantity Sweet Pastry (see recipe page 152)

FILLING

6 oz/175 g unsalted butter, chopped

1¾ cups (6 oz/175 g) ground almonds

¾ cup (6 oz/175 g) superfine/caster sugar

7 oz/200 g dark chocolate (70% couverture)

3 eggs

1 x 14 oz/400 g can pears in syrup, quartered

Treacle and Lemon Tart

I love treacle tart! It reminds me of home and it is one of my go-to dishes whenever I'm feeling a little homesick. My tart doesn't include breadcrumbs so is less heavy than normal but just as delicious. Serve with Orange and Date Cream (page 164).

SERVES 8–10

1 quantity Sweet Pastry (see recipe
    page 152)

FILLING

12 tablespoons golden syrup

zest of 1½ lemons

1 oz/30 g unsalted butter

6 tablespoons single/thickened
    cream

4 eggs

Firstly, you will need to make Sweet Pastry or buy a pre-made and pre-cooked shortcrust tart case from the shops.

If making your own pastry, blind bake it as per the recipe instructions and leave it to cool in the tin.

Preheat the oven to 320°F/160°C.

Place the golden syrup, lemon zest, butter and cream in a saucepan and warm over a low heat until the butter has melted and all the ingredients have combined. Remove the pan from the heat.

With a hand whisk, lightly whisk the eggs until combined.

When the mixture is cool, add the eggs and stir to combine.

Pour the mixture into the cooled tart case. The filling should come almost to the top.

Bake in the oven for 35–40 minutes or until golden and just firm to the touch.

Remove from the oven and serve warm with a dollop of Orange and Date Cream (page 164).

Nutella and Banana Tart

These next two recipes are great last-minute desserts as they take only a matter of minutes to make and are gorgeous served warm with homemade ice-cream.

MOTHER RECIPE

SERVES 6—8

1 sheet pre-rolled puff pastry

1 small jar Nutella spread

3–4 ripe bananas

2 teaspoons unsalted butter, melted

Preheat the oven to 400°F/200°C.

Line a baking tray, large enough for the pastry sheet to fit, with baking paper.

Place 1 sheet of the frozen pastry onto the centre of the baking paper and leave for 10 minutes to thaw.

Meanwhile, slice the bananas into ½ in (1 cm) rounds.

With the back of a knife, gently score a ½ in (1 cm) line around the outside of the pastry (don't cut all the way through the pastry). This will form the outside of the tart wall.

With a fork, prick some holes in the centre square of the pastry (not the outer wall) a dozen times.

Using a blunt knife, spread the Nutella into the centre square of the pastry being careful not to get any on the outside wall. Ensure that the Nutella is spread evenly and is about ⅕ in (3–5 mm) thick.

Starting at one end of the pastry and finishing at the other, arrange the banana slices in the centre square on top of the Nutella.

Using a pastry brush (or the back of a spoon if you don't have one) brush the wall of the pastry with the melted butter.

Place the tart in the oven and cook for 25–30 minutes or until the walls of the tart are golden.

Once cooked, remove the tart from the oven, cut into desired-sized portions and serve with a dollop of Chocolate and Honeycomb Ice-cream (page 136).

Apple and Cinnamon Tart

DAUGHTER RECIPE

SERVES 6—8

1 sheet pre-rolled puff pastry

3 green apples, peeled and cored,
   any variety will do

¼ cup brown sugar

½ teaspoon ground cinnamon

½ oz/15 g unsalted butter, melted

Preheat the oven to 400°F/200°C.

Line a baking tray with baking paper, large enough for the pastry sheet to fit.

Place the sheet of the frozen pastry onto the centre of the baking paper and leave for 10 minutes to thaw.

Meanwhile, slice the apples thinly, about $^1/_5$ in (3 mm) thick, and place them in a bowl.

Sprinkle the sugar and cinnamon onto the apples and toss the apples around so they are coated in the sugar mix.

With the back of a knife, gently score a ½ in (1 cm) line around the outside of the pastry (be careful not to cut all the way through the pastry). This will form the outside of the tart wall.

With a fork, score the centre square of the pastry (not the outer wall) a dozen times.

Starting at one end of the pastry and finishing at the other, arrange the apple slices in the centre square, ensuring that there are no gaps.

Using a pastry brush (or the back of a spoon if you don't have one), brush the top of the apple slices and also the walls of the pastry with the melted butter.

Sprinkle an additional tablespoon of sugar onto the apple slices.

Place in the oven and cook for 25—30 minutes or until the pastry is golden and the apples are cooked through.

Once cooked, remove the tart from the oven, cut into desired-sized portions and serve with a dollop of Vanilla Ice-cream (page 134).

Mini Doughnuts

These remind me of long road trips in the UK with my family. If I was lucky we'd stop at one of the cafes along the way for 'dunkin doughnuts'—bite-sized pieces of doughnuts dipped in warm chocolate sauce. These are a great dessert to share and are amazingly good dipped in Hot Chocolate Sauce (page 161) or served with Vanilla Ice-cream (page 134).

SERVES 3—4

Pour the vegetable oil into a large wok or saucepan and heat over a medium to high heat.

Sieve the flour and sugar into a small bowl.

Place the cold water and butter into a saucepan and place on a high heat.

When the butter has melted and the water is at a rapid boil remove the pan from the heat and quickly add the flour and sugar mix. Stir the mixture quickly with a wooden spoon until a smooth paste forms.

Place the mixture into an electric mixer and leave to cool for 15 minutes.

Lightly hand whisk the eggs until combined.

Put the electric mixer onto a medium to low speed and, using the beater attachment, slowly add the eggs one spoonful at a time, ensuring the egg is combined before adding the next spoonful. Once the egg has been added the mixture should be glossy and smooth.

To test to see if the now-heated oil is the right temperature, drop a bit of dough into the oil. If it sizzles and spits and the dough burns before it is cooked through then lower the heat. If the dough sits in the oil and doesn't seem to be cooking turn the heat up, or wait a bit longer until the oil is hotter and then test the oil again. You are looking for a slight sizzle around the dough.

Using two oiled spoons, form the dough into small oval-shaped balls.

4 cups (2 pints/1 litre) vegetable oil

1 cup (5½ oz/160 g) all-purpose/plain flour

1 teaspoon superfine/caster sugar

½ cup (4 fl oz/125 ml) cold water

1¾ oz/50 g unsalted butter, cut into cubes

2 eggs

superfine/caster sugar, for coating

Using a slotted spoon, one at a time, carefully lower the dough balls into the hot oil. Remove the balls carefully from the oil once golden and cooked through. You may need to do this in batches.

Place the cooked dough balls on kitchen towel to remove some of the oil then roll them in caster sugar. You can also add a pinch of cinnamon to the sugar if you want to make cinnamon doughnuts.

Serve warm with Hot Chocolate Sauce (see recipe page 161).

Note: When the oil has completely cooled you can pour it back into the container so you can use it again at a later date. Perhaps for the Toffee Bananas (page 133)?

Apple Strudel

A gorgeous, warming pudding, the perfect ending for a long rainy Sunday lunch. Delicious served with Cardamom and Coconut Ice-cream (see recipe page 135).

SERVES 6

2 sheets 8 x 8 in (20 x 20 cm) pre-rolled frozen puff pastry

½ cup (2 oz/60 g) fresh breadcrumbs

2 oz/60 g unsalted butter

3–4 apples, peeled, cored and thinly sliced (about 15 oz/450 g)

½ cup (3 oz/90 g) raisins

¼ cup (2 oz/60 g) superfine/caster sugar

zest of 1 lemon

1 teaspoon ground cinnamon

1 oz/30 g butter, melted

Preheat the oven to 350°F/180°C. Line a large baking tray with baking paper.

Thaw the two sheets of frozen pastry.

In a large frying pan, fry the breadcrumbs in the butter over a medium–high heat. At first the breadcrumbs will look too wet but keep stirring and they will soon crisp up.

Once the breadcrumbs are crisp and golden, add to the frying pan the sliced apples, raisins, sugar, lemon zest and ground cinnamon.

Cook for 5–10 minutes over a low heat until the sugar has melted and the apple slices have started to soften.

Place the two thawed pastry sheets onto the pre-lined baking tray, lapping one about an inch over the other so as to make one long sheet of pastry. Seal the pastry sheets together with your fingertips.

Spread the filling over the pastry, ensuring the entire sheet is covered and then roll the pastry up vertically, like a swiss roll.

Brush the pastry with the melted butter and bake in the oven for 25–35 minutes or until golden and cooked through.

Once cooked, remove the strudel from the oven and serve.

Bread and Butter Pudding with Pear and Raisins

A good old-fashioned British pudding made more delicious with the introduction of some added ingredients. This pudding lends itself to all sorts of fruits so why not try it with apples, berries or whatever you have left over in your fruit bowl?! Serve with Vanilla Ice-cream (page 134).

SERVES 6—8

Preheat the oven to 350°F/180°C.

Grease a 11¾ x 11¾ in (30 x 30 cm) ovenproof dish with butter.

Remove the crust from the bread and generously butter one side of each slice. Cut the bread slices in half diagonally to make triangles.

In a saucepan, combine the milk and cream and warm over a low heat. Do not allow the liquid to come to a simmer.

Gently whisk the eggs and sugar until combined.

Add the lukewarm milk mixture to the eggs, a little at the start, and mix to combine until the sugar melts.

Place the bread in the dish in layers around the outside of the dish (with the top of the bread triangle at the top and the buttered side facing in), working your way into the middle of the dish and adding the zest, sliced pears and raisins between the layers as you go, until all the ingredients have been used. Alternatively, you can layer the bread from the bottom of the dish, sprinkling the zest, pears and raisins in between each layer.

Once all the ingredients have been used, pour the milk mixture over the top. This should come three-quarters of the way up the bread. You may not need it all.

Bake in the oven for 30—40 minutes or until the bread has browned on the top.

Once cooked, remove from the oven and serve warm.

1 large loaf of white bread (pre-sliced)

4 oz/125 g unsalted butter, soft

2 cups (17½ fl oz/500 ml) milk

1 cup (9½ oz/270 g) single/thickened cream

4 egg yolks

1 egg white

2 cups (16 oz/480 g) superfine/caster sugar

zest of 1 lemon

3 pears, peeled and cut into finger-sized slices (you can use apples or any other fruit)

½ cup (2½ oz/75 g) raisins

Chocolate Lava Pudding

Super easy to make, this dessert has to be in my top five! You can make individual portions but the bigger the better as far as I am concerned. The gooey centre is imperative so make sure you watch it carefully in the oven. Serve with a handful of berries and a mound of Vanilla Ice-cream (page 134) and it will make your top five too!

SERVES 8—10

5 oz/150 g unsalted butter, roughly chopped

8 oz/225 g dark chocolate (70% couverture), broken into pieces

1 cup (8½ oz/240 g) superfine/caster sugar

4 eggs, lightly beaten

1 tablespoon all-purpose/plain flour

Preheat the oven to 350°F/180°C.

Put the butter and chocolate in a saucepan and place over a medium to low heat until melted. Once melted, remove the pan from the heat and leave to cool.

Whisk the eggs and sugar together until combined.

Once cool, add the sugar mixture to the chocolate and stir thoroughly to combine. Add the flour and stir.

Pour into an ovenproof 8 x 8 in (20 x 20 cm) dish and place in the oven for 15—25 minutes. Once cooked, the pudding should be set around the edges but still have a little wobble in the centre.

Serve warm.

Toffee Bananas

This is another great dessert to share with friends and family. These crunchy banana pieces are delicious with Cardamom and Coconut Ice-cream (page 135).

SERVES 2—4

Peel and cut the bananas into 1 in (2 cm) pieces.

To make the batter, mix together all the batter ingredients.

Heat the oil in a large, deep frying pan or wok. The oil will need to be 350°F/180°C. If you do not have a thermometer you can test the heat of the oil by dropping a large breadcrumb into the oil, when it goes golden brown this is a good time to start frying your banana pieces.

Fill a large bowl with iced water.

Coat the banana pieces in the batter and carefully fry them in the hot oil until golden brown. Using tongs, carefully remove them from the oil and place them onto kitchen paper. You will need to do this in batches, setting the batches aside until they are all cooked.

For the toffee, add the water and sugar to a deep saucepan and boil until it turns a dark golden colour (should take about 5 minutes). Do not stir until the desired colour is reached and then remove the pan from the heat and stir with a wooden spoon.

Skewer a banana piece in the centre with a skewer or sharp knife, then carefully lower it into the hot toffee, coating it all over.

Once coated, quickly plunge the toffee banana piece into the bowl of iced water and leave it there for a few seconds to set. Once set remove and drain well. Repeat this process with the rest of the banana pieces.

Once all the banana pieces are coated, sprinkle on the sesame seeds and serve.

Note: When the oil has completely cooled you can pour it back into the container so you can use it again at a later date. Perhaps for the Mini Doughnuts (page 123)?

2 bananas (not too ripe)

4 cups (2 pints/1 litre) vegetable/ sunflower or canola oil

1 tablespoon sesame seeds, lightly toasted

BATTER

1 tablespoon self-rising/self-raising flour

1 tablespoon rice flour

1 tablespoon cornstarch/cornflour

pinch salt

pinch sugar

3 tablespoons water

TOFFEE

1 cup (8½ oz/240 g) superfine/caster sugar

¼ cup (2 fl oz/60 ml) water

Vanilla Ice-cream

I can never have enough ice-cream in the freezer, for me it is a staple. Whether served on its own, with a sauce or alongside a tart or pudding, ice-cream is a necessity! For many, ice-cream means making custard and purchasing ice-cream machines. While this traditional technique produces an amazing result there are other, easier ways to make it. Here are a few options for you to try. They are gorgeously creamy, so sample these and you may never buy ice-cream again!

MOTHER RECIPE

SERVES 6—8

2 cups (19 oz/540 g) double cream

1 cup (1 x 14 oz/395 g tin) condensed milk

1 vanilla bean, deseeded or
1 teaspoon vanilla paste

Place all the ingredients into a mixing bowl and whisk (by hand or in an electric mixer) until very soft peaks form. Be very careful not to over whisk it.

Pour the mixture into a container, cover and place in the freezer overnight or until set (it should take about 5—6 hours). Serve with sauces and toppings of your choice.

Cardamom and Coconut Ice-cream

DAUGHTER RECIPE

SERVES 6—8

Place the cream, condensed milk and cardamom into a mixing bowl and whisk (by hand or in an electric mixer) until very soft peaks form. Be very careful not to over whisk it.

Fold the grated coconut into the cream mixture.

Pour the mixture into a container, cover and place in the freezer overnight or until set (it should take about 5—6 hours). Serve with sauces and toppings of your choice

2 cups (19 oz/540 g) double cream

1 cup (1 x 14 oz/395 g tin) condensed milk

1 teaspoon ground cardamom

1 cup (2 oz/65 g) grated coconut

Vanilla and Lemon Curd Ice-cream

DAUGHTER RECIPE

SERVES 6—8

Place the cream and the condensed milk into a mixing bowl and whisk (by hand or in an electric mixer) until very soft peaks form. Be very careful not to over whisk it.

Make the curd by mixing the lemon juice and condensed milk together until it thickens.

Pour half of the cream mixture into a plastic container. Pour over the lemon curd and spread it so it covers the cream. Fill the container with the remainder of the cream mixture. Alternatively, you could pour all of the cream mixture into a plastic container and swirl in the lemon curd mixture.

Place in the freezer overnight or until set and then serve.

2 cups (19 oz/540 g) double cream

1 cup (1 x 14 oz/395 g tin) condensed milk

LEMON CURD

1 cup (4 oz/125 ml) lemon juice, sieved

½ cup (7 oz/200 g) condensed milk

Chocolate and Honeycomb Ice-cream

DAUGHTER RECIPE

SERVES 6—8

2 cups (19 oz/540 g) double cream

1 cup (1 x 14 oz/395 g tin) condensed
milk

3 medium-sized honeycomb
chocolate bars

Place the cream and condensed milk into a mixing bowl and whisk
(by hand or in an electric mixer) until very soft peaks form. Be very
careful not to over whisk it.

Break up the honeycomb bars in a pestle and mortar (if you
haven't got one of these place them in a zip lock bag and use the end
of a rolling pin to crush them) until the pieces are small.

Fold the pieces of the honeycomb bar into the cream mixture.

Pour the mixture into a container, cover and place in the freezer
overnight or until set (it should take about 5—6 hours).

Serve this with Mars Bar Sauce (see recipe page 154).

Strawberry Ice-cream

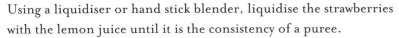

DAUGHTER RECIPE

SERVES 6

Using a liquidiser or hand stick blender, liquidise the strawberries with the lemon juice until it is the consistency of a puree.

Add the cream and icing sugar and continue to liquidise for 45 seconds until it is well combined.

Place the mixture into a container and freeze overnight or until set and then serve.

9 oz/250 g strawberries

½ cup lemon juice

2/3 cup (6 oz/180 g) double cream

1½ cups (11¾ oz/335 g) confectioner's/icing sugar

Petits Fours

Chocolate Discs

These are the easiest-ever chocolates to make and the topping options are endless—let your imagination run wild. Here are a few of my favourites.

MOTHER RECIPE

MAKES 12—14

7 oz/200 g dark chocolate (70% couverture), roughly chopped

1 tablespoon flaked almonds

1 tablespoon hazelnuts, roughly chopped

1 tablespoon raisins

Line a baking tray with baking paper.

Place the chocolate pieces into a heatproof bowl and put on top of a saucepan of barely simmering water.

Stir the chocolate over the heat until half of the chocolate has melted. Remove from the bowl from the heat and keep stirring until the remainder of the chocolate has melted.

Place the nuts into a small frying pan and dry roast them until they are golden.

Using a tablespoon, make discs of the liquid chocolate on the baking paper, using the back of the spoon to shape and flatten the chocolate. They need to be $^1/_5$ in (5 mm) in height. Do this until all the chocolate is used up.

Scatter over the roasted nuts and raisins, pressing them down gently in the chocolate.

Place the lined baking tray in the fridge until the chocolates have set before serving.

Chocolate, Nuts and Sea Salt Discs

DAUGHTER RECIPE

MAKES 12—14

7 oz/200 g dark chocolate (70% couverture), roughly chopped

1 tablespoon flaked almonds

1 tablespoon hazelnuts, roughly chopped

sea salt flakes (small pinch for each disc)

Line a baking tray with baking paper.

Place the chocolate pieces into a heatproof bowl and put on top of a saucepan of barely simmering water.

Stir the chocolate over the heat until half of the chocolate has melted. Remove the bowl from the heat and keep stirring until the remainder of the chocolate has melted.

Place the nuts into a small frying pan and dry roast them until they are golden.

Using a tablespoon, make discs of the liquid chocolate on the baking paper, using the back of the spoon to shape and flatten the chocolate. They need to be $1/5$ in (5 mm) in height. Do this until all the chocolate is used up.

Scatter over the roasted nuts, pressing them down gently in the chocolate.

Sprinkle a small pinch of the salt on each of the discs.

Place the lined baking tray in the fridge until the chocolates have set before serving.

Chocolate Orange Discs

DAUGHTER RECIPE

SERVES 12—14

Line a baking tray with baking paper.

Place the chocolate pieces into a heatproof bowl and put on top of a saucepan of barely simmering water.

Stir the chocolate over the heat until half of the chocolate has melted. Remove the bowl from the heat and keep stirring until the remainder of the chocolate has melted.

Add the finely grated orange zest to the melted chocolate and stir to combine.

Using a tablespoon, make discs of the liquid chocolate on the baking paper, using the back of the spoon to shape and flatten the chocolate. They need to be $1/5$ in (5 mm) in height. Do this until all the chocolate is used up.

Place the lined baking tray in the fridge until the chocolates have set before serving.

7 oz/200 g dark chocolate (70% couverture), roughly chopped
zest of 1 orange, finely grated

Rocky Road Discs

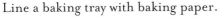

DAUGHTER RECIPE

MAKES 12—14

Line a baking tray with baking paper.

Place the chocolate pieces into a heatproof bowl and put on top of a saucepan of barely simmering water.

Stir the chocolate over the heat until half of the chocolate has melted. Remove from the bowl from the heat and keep stirring until the remainder of the chocolate has melted.

Place the peanuts into a small frying pan and dry roast them until they are golden.

Using a tablespoon, make discs of the liquid chocolate on the baking paper, using the back of the spoon to shape and flatten the chocolate. They need to be $^1/_5$ in (5 mm) in height. Do this until all the chocolate is used up.

Scatter over the roasted nuts, marshmallows and raisins, pressing them down gently in the chocolate.

Place the lined baking tray in the fridge until the chocolates have set before serving.

7 oz/200 g dark chocolate (70% couverture), roughly chopped

1 tablespoon peanuts (roughly chopped)

1 tablespoon mini marshmallows

1 tablespoon raisins

Chocolate Biscuit Truffles

MAKES 24—26

16 graham crackers/digestive biscuits, crushed (about 9 oz/250 g)

1¾ oz/50 g unsalted butter, finely diced

1 tablespoon cocoa powder

1 cup (5 oz/140 g) confectioner's/icing sugar

2 tablespoons single/thickened cream

4 drops vanilla essence

cocoa powder, for dusting

Use a pestle and mortar to crush the crackers until fine crumbs form. Or place the biscuits in a zip lock bag and crush them with the end of a rolling pin.

Add the butter to the crumbs, rubbing it in with your hands so it is evenly distributed.

Sift in the cocoa and icing sugar.

Pour in the cream and vanilla essence, stirring to combine all the ingredients until a stiff paste forms.

Roll the mixture into evenly sized balls (about the size of a Ferrero Rocher) with your hands.

Then roll the balls through sieved cocoa powder until fully covered. Shake off the excess.

Place truffles in a sealed container until needed. Best served at room temperature.

Baking Basics

Sweet Pastry

MAKES ENOUGH FOR A 9 IN/22 CM ROUND TART CASE

4 oz/125 g unsalted butter, cold and diced

6 oz/185 g all-purpose/plain flour

1 tablespoon confectioner's/icing sugar, sifted

Preheat oven to 350°F/180°C.

Place all the ingredients into a food processor and pulse until fine crumbs form. If you don't have a food processor, rub the cold butter into the flour and confectioner's sugar with your fingers, until the mixture resembles bread crumbs.

Press the crumbs directly into a 9 in (22 cm) round tart case with your hands, pressing down with your fingers firmly until the crumbs start to form one layer. The layer needs to be about $\frac{1}{5}$ in (3 mm) thick. Start with the base of the tin and work your way up the sides.

Place the tart in the fridge for 1 hour.

Blind bake the pastry by putting the baking tray in the oven for 25 minutes or until golden and the pastry starts to come away from the sides of the case. No baking beads are needed for this step.

Remove the pastry from the oven and leave it to cool before pouring in the filling of your choice.

Flaky Pastry

MAKES ENOUGH FOR 12 ECCLES CAKES

Place the butter in the freezer.

Sift the flour and salt into a large bowl. Once the butter is hard, using a microplane (or small grater), grate it into the bowl with the flour. Mix the butter into the flour as you go so it doesn't stick together too much.

With a sharp kitchen knife, cut into the mixture until fine crumbs form.

Add enough cold water (a little at a time) to form a dough. It should not be wet.

With your hands mix the crumbs together to form the dough into a disc, wrap it in plastic wrap and place in the fridge for 30 minutes before using.

5 oz/150 g unsalted butter

1¼ cups (7 oz/200 g) all-purpose/ plain flour

pinch of salt

2 tablespoons cold water

Note: Flaky pastry is a beautifully light pastry that melts in the mouth. Also an ideal pastry to use when making sausage rolls.

Mars Bar Sauce

I cannot eat ice-cream without this sauce. Try it, you will not be disappointed!

MOTHER RECIPE

SERVES 4

2 king-size Mars Bars

milk (full cream or semi-skimmed will do)

Roughly break the Mars Bars into a saucepan.

Add one tablespoon of milk to the saucepan and heat on a medium to low heat, stirring continuously. Keep adding the milk, 1 tablespoon at a time, stirring between additions until the desired consistency is reached (I like mine quite thick).

When the chocolate is melted and only small pieces of the nougat remain, remove the pan from the heat. These pieces will go really chewy when served with cold ice-cream.

Serve while still warm.

Note: Any leftover sauce can be placed in a sterilised jar in the fridge and reheated at a later date (it will keep for about a week).

Snickers Sauce

DAUGHTER RECIPE

SERVES 4

2 king-size Snickers bars

milk (full cream or semi-skimmed will
do)

Roughly break the Snickers bars into a saucepan.

Add one tablespoon of milk to the saucepan and heat on a medium to low heat, stirring continuously. Keep adding the milk, 1 tablespoon at a time, stirring between additions until the desired consistency is reached (I like mine quite thick).

When the chocolate is melted and only small pieces of the nougat remain, remove the pan from the heat. These pieces will go really chewy when served with cold ice-cream.

Serve while still warm.

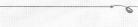

Butterscotch Sauce

SERVES 4—5

Put all the ingredients in a pan over a medium—low heat and stir until the butter has melted and the sugar has dissolved.

Serve while warm.

1¾ oz/50 g butter

1⅓ cups (9½ oz/270 g) brown sugar

⅔ cup (6 oz/ 170 g) single/thickened cream

Note: Any leftover sauce can be placed in a sterilised jar in the fridge and reheated at a later date (it will keep for about a week).

Caramel Sauce

SERVES 4—5

Combine the sugar and water in a high-sided saucepan and place on a low heat until the sugar dissolves (do not stir).

Once the sugar has melted, turn the heat up to medium and heat until it reaches a dark caramel colour.

At this stage, remove the pan from the heat and carefully pour in the cream, stirring with a wooden spoon until combined. Be careful as the mixture will froth upwards and spit.

Serve while still warm.

¾ cup superfine/caster sugar

¼ cup water

½ cup (4 oz/125 g) single/thickened cream

Note: Any leftover sauce can be placed in a sterilised jar in the fridge and reheated at a later date (it will keep for about a week).

Salted Caramel Sauce

SERVES 10—12

Heat the sugar in a large pan over a medium to high heat, whisking as the sugar melts. It will clump together but don't worry, keep whisking and it will eventually dissolve. Continue to heat the sugar until it reaches a dark amber colour.

Whisk in the salt and then all the butter at once until the butter is melted. Be careful as the mixture will froth up a bit.

Remove the pan from the heat and add the cream, stirring until the sauce is smooth.

Serve while still warm.

Note: Any leftover sauce can be placed in a sterilised jar in the fridge and reheated at a later date (it will keep for about a week).

1 cup superfine/caster sugar

1 teaspoon sea salt (it needs to be fine granules)

5 oz/150 g unsalted butter, at room temperature and cut into cubes

⅔ cup (6 oz/170 g) double cream, at room temperature

Hot Chocolate Sauce

SERVES 8—10

Pour the cream into a saucepan and heat over a low to medium heat until simmering gently.

Remove from the heat, add the chocolate pieces and stir until all the chocolate is melted.

Add the butter and stir until thoroughly combined.

Serve while still warm.

Note: Any leftover sauce can be placed in a sterilised jar in the fridge and reheated at a later date (it will keep for about a week).

1 cup single/thickened cream

7 oz/200 g dark chocolate (70% couverture), roughly chopped

¾ oz/25 g unsalted butter, cut into cubes

Chantilly Cream

Why serve your puddings with a normal pouring cream when you can create these beauties in just a few moments. Amazing!

MOTHER RECIPE

SERVES 10—20

1 cup (7½ oz/235 g) single/thickened cream

¼ cup (1¼ oz/35g) confectioner's/icing sugar, sifted

1 vanilla pod (or 1 teaspoon vanilla extract/paste)

Combine the cream and icing sugar in an electric mixer.

Add the vanilla pod or extract/paste.

On a medium speed, whisk the mixture until soft peaks form. Be careful not to over whisk it.

Serve or place in fridge until required.

Orange and Date Cream

DAUGHTER RECIPE

SERVES 10–20

juice of 1 orange

5 dates, pitted and roughly chopped

1 cup (7½ oz/235 g) single/thickened cream

¼ cup confectioner's/icing sugar, sifted

Place the orange juice and dates in a saucepan. Bring to boil over a high heat and then drop to a low heat and simmer for 5 minutes. Break down the date pieces with the back of a wooden spoon and leave to cool.

Combine the cream and icing sugar in an electric mixer.

On a medium speed, whisk the mixture until soft peaks form. Be careful not to over whisk it.

Once the orange/date mixture is cool, spoon the dates (not the excess liquid) into the whipped cream and fold them together until just combined. You want to see chunks of the date syrup swirled through the cream.

Serve or place in fridge until required.

Raspberry Jam Cream

Combine the cream and icing sugar in an electric mixer.

On a medium speed whisk the mixture until soft peaks form. Be careful not to over whisk it.

Fold the raspberry jam into the whipped cream until just combined. You want to see swirls of the jam through the cream.

Serve or place in fridge until required.

1 cup (7½ oz/235 g) single/thickened cream

¼ cup confectioner's/icing sugar, sifted

2 tablespoons raspberry jam (you can use strawberry, blueberry or even apricot jam)

Recipe index

Acknowledgements

There are so many people in my life to thank for helping me put this book together.

To my friends, the inspirers, the supporters, the proof readers (who turned electrical currents into the edible dried fruit), the recipe checkers and the taste testers, thank you for all your help. I hope the added sugar to your daily diet didn't add too much to your waist lines!

Thank you to MercerBell, my employer, for supporting me throughout my MasterChef adventure and to my new found MasterChef friends who made the experience so very memorable.

To my amazing family, thank you for always being there for me and inspiring me. I know you can't choose your family but if I could, I would choose you, every single time.

And lastly to my gorgeous husband, Sammy. Thank you for believing in me and encouraging me to follow my dreams. You have earned a lifetime of brownie points! I love you, always and forever. xxxx

First published in 2014 by New Holland Publishers Pty Ltd
London • Sydney • Cape Town • Auckland

The Chandlery Unit 114 50 Westminster Bridge Road London SE1 7QY United Kingdom
1/66 Gibbes Street Chatswood NSW 2067 Australia
Wembley Square First Floor Solan Road Gardens Cape Town 8001 South Africa
218 Lake Road Northcote Auckland New Zealand

www.newhollandpublishers.com

A record of this book is held at the British Library and the National Library of Australia.

ISBN 9781742575162

Managing director: Fiona Schultz
Publisher: Diane Ward
Project editor: Jodi De Vantier
Designer: Tracy Loughlin
Photographs: Sue Stubbs
Food stylist: Arum Shim
Proofreader: Vicky Fisher
Production director: Olga Dementiev
Printer: Toppan Leefung Printing Ltd (China)

10 9 8 7 6 5 4 3 2 1

Our thanks to: Mud Australia, Plenty Kitchen and Tableware and Burnt Orange for props.

Keep up with New Holland Publishers on Facebook
www.facebook.com/NewHollandPublishers